# Micro:bit IoT In C

**Harry Fairhead**

**I/O Press**
**I Programmer Library**

Harry Fairhead, Micro:bit IoT In C

ISBN Paperback: 978-1-871962-45-1

First Edition
First Printing, 2016
Revision 0

Published by IO Press                www.iopress.info
In association with I Programmer     www.i-programmer.info
and with I o T Programmer            www.iot-programmer.com

The publisher recognizes and respects all marks used by companies and manufacturers as a means to distinguish their products. All brand names and product names mentioned in this book are trade marks or service marks of their respective companies and our omission of trade marks is not an attempt to infringe on the property of others.

In particular we acknowledge that "BBC" and "micro:bit" are trade marks of the BBC.

# Preface

The BBC micro:bit is a remarkable device capable of taking on a variety of roles. Initially it was the preserve of school children, with one million given away free via secondary schools in the UK and the emphasis was on introducing this audience to programming and digital technology. Now it has gone on public sale and the fact that it is an ideal vehicle for IoT can come to the fore.

To realize its full potential as an IoT device, we need to look outside the coding environments provided by its own website. As an mbed device, the micro:bit is capable of being programmed in C which gives you full access to its features and to external devices. The main reason for choosing C is speed which is crucial when you are writing programs to communicate with the outside world.

This book isn't an introduction to the micro:bit. For this you are recommended to visit its own website, https://www.microbit.co.uk/ where you will find activities with step-by-step guidance for beginners. Instead this book assumes you have taken you first steps with programming, have an interest in electronics and want to experiment with the exciting features provided by the micro:bit.

After writing a first "Hello Blinky" C program with the mbed online compiler, we move to the desktop to using an offline approach using the yotta development environment plus NetBeans to make things even easier. Now we are ready to discover how to control the micro:bit's I/O lines, exploring the basis of using the GPIO. For speed, however, we need to work directly with the raw hardware and also master memory mapping, pulse width modulation and other more sophisticated bus types.

From here we can start connecting sensors using first the I2C bus, then by implementing a custom protocol for a one-wire bus, and eventually adding eight channels of 12-bit AtoD with the SPI bus, which involves overcoming some subtle difficulties. We then look at serial connections, one of the oldest ways of connecting devices but still very useful. The micro: bit lacks WiFi connectivity but using a low-cost device we enable a connection to the Internet via its serial port which allows it to become a server.

Finally we look at the micro:bit's LED display. This may only be 5x5, but it is very versatile, especially when you use pulse width modulation to vary the brightness level, something we demonstrate in a classic game, written of course in C.

For updates, errata, links to resources and the source code for the programs in this book visit its dedicated page on the IoT Programmer website:

http://www.iot-programmer.com/index.php/books/micro-bit-iot-in-c

# Table of Contents

# Chapter 1

# Getting Started With C/C++

Anyone who wants to use the BBC micro:bit to its full potential as an IoT device needs to look outside the coding environments provided by its own website. Fortunately as an mbed device, the micro:bit is capable of being programmed in C/C++. Here we look at how to use the mbed online compiler for a simple demo program.

## Setting Up an Mbed Device

The fact that the micro:bit is an mbed device brings with it both good and not so good news. The good news is that you can program the micro:bit in C/C++. The bad news is that the documentation only gives you a hint as to how to do it. Here we explore how to use the online compiler. In the next chapter we'll find out how to do the same job offline using NetBeans. While I'm specifically looking at the micro:bit, much of this will apply to any mbed device.

If you want to get started with C/C++ on the micro:bit quickly and don't mind signing up to an online service then it is all very easy. On the other hand, if you have a preference for a desktop IDE, or just a command line interface things are a bit more difficult. The reason is that mbed comes with a brand new **make** replacement called **yotta**. It's not that yotta is bad, it is just another thing to learn. It is also surprising how complicated embedded programming has become - so much so that it actually need something this complicated. We seem to be a long way from the C programming running on almost bare metal. Once upon a time the hardware was the tough part, now it's the software as well.

So if you want an easy life go for the online compiler. If you want more control, but perhaps more complexity, go for the offline approach. Personally, I prefer the offline approach using NetBeans and suggest that after you have tried things out with the online compiler you spend a few hours getting things set up for NetBeans development, which is described in the next chapter.

## Why C/C++?

Before you spend time finding out how to program in C/C++ there is the good question of why bother? After all, the micro:bit's own website offers the choice of Touch Develop, JavaScript and MicroPython to program it and they are all fairly easy to use.

The answer to the question of why C/C++ is that it gets you closest to the hardware. Not all of the features and facilities of the micro:bit are accessible from the higher level languages. For example, at the moment you can't get access to the micro:bit's radio. Using C/C++ and the microbit library you can use the BlueTooth radio as a simple point to point radio connection between micro:bits. This makes it possible to build radio control robots and similar gadgets, something much harder if all of the connections have to go through the BlueTooth stack. Another example is the LED control. In MicroPython you have nine brightness levels. In the micro:bit's other supplied languages the LEDs are either on or off. In C/C++ you can set any of 255 levels.

Going beyond the standard hardware you can also implement missing hardware facilities. For example, there is no SPI bus available under any of the supplied languages, only an I2C bus. Using C/C++ you can access a standard mbed SPI driver and work with SPI peripherals. You can even use your own code to implement protocols that are not supported such as the one-wire bus and the DHT11/22 temperature humidity sensor.

The reason you can implement these additional protocols is that C/C++ is about as fast as you can get on any machine. You might be able to get some more speed out of an assembly language version of a program, but it would only be a few percent. Using C/C++ lets your programs run tens of times faster. For example, the blinky program given below runs about 20 times faster than the equivalent MicroPython program. When you are writing embedded programs often speed really does matter. You might not be able to write it in MicroPython and have to move to C/C++. If you can't write it in C/C++ then there is a good chance it can't be done using the hardware you have.

C/C++ isn't significantly harder to work with than other languages. C is particularly simple and easy to use. The micro:bit library is written in C++, but for most of the time you can make use of it in a dialect of C which is quite good enough for the task.

# The Online Compiler

The online compiler for the micro:bit is the best way to get started. At the time of writing, you have to go to the mbed Classic Developer site to find it, but this could change.

To use it you have to sign up for an account with mbed at:

**https://www.mbed.com/**

Once you have an account and have signed in, your first task is to get the compiler set up with the micro:bit as its target. One route is to go to Platforms and select BBC as the vendor.

There is only one product in that category, i.e. the micro:bit

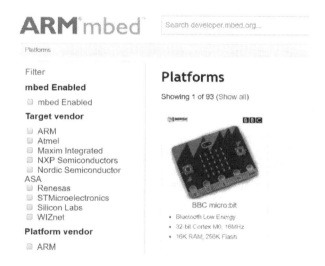

Alternatively you can go to the compiler and select the target device icon in the top right, which initially shows as "No device Selected". Click the Add Platform button and you are back to the Platform selection page. Select the BBC micro:bit and you are back in the same place.

The micro:bit page contains a lot of information but if you just want to work with it in the compiler simply select the Add to your mbed Compiler at the right of the screen:

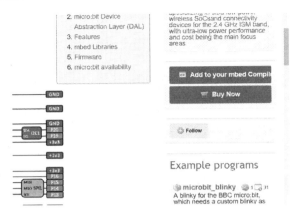

Following this when you go back to the compiler you will see the BBC micro:bit as the target platform in the top right hand corner:

## Hello Blinky

You are now ready to start work on a project but at the moment there isn't a good starter project template. However Lancaster University has provided a template called Blinky to flash an LED, the equivalent of a Hello World program for the device.

There are two ways to work with the micro:bit - as a pure mbed device or using the library or framework, built by Lancaster University. As long as you don't want to change to a different device, the Lancaster framework is the one to use. The mbed library makes it easy to write a single program that will work on different hardware and this is its big advantage. You can use the mbed library with the micro:bit, but unless you really do want to move to another piece of hardware it is better to use the micro:bit library.

To get a starter project you have to select the Samples template because the blinky templates use the mbed library.

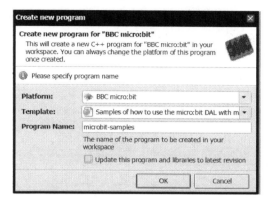

It takes some time to build the project but eventually you will see the finished project ready for you to edit.

The C/C++ programs are all in the source directory as usual, but the difference is that you are using the microbit framework rather than the usual mbed library.

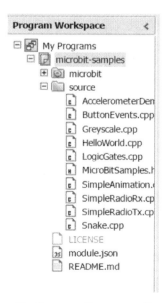

If you want to you can compile (ignore the compiler warnings) and run the sample without modification just to check everything works. If you select the compile button the program is compiled and then downloaded to your machine.

You then have to download the file

```
microbit-samples_NRF51_MICROBIT.hex
```

to the micro:bit via the usb drive in the usual way. When you run the program you will discover that by default you will see a Hello World message scroll across the screen.

If you want to see any of the other demos in action, simply open the MicroBitSamples.h file and uncomment the line corresponding to the one you want to run.

## Your First Program

At the moment the samples provide the best starting template for you own projects. Create a new project based on the samples template and call it **pulsetest**.

Next delete all of the source files in the Source directory. The quickest way to do this is to delete the Source directory and then add it back as a new directory. Create a new file called main.cpp - you can call it anything you like but the name **main** gives you the clue that it is the start of the program.

Enter the following code:

```cpp
#include "MicroBit.h"
MicroBit uBit; int main() {
 uBit.init();
 uBit.display.scroll("NEW PROGRAM");
 while (1) {
  uBit.io.P0.setDigitalValue(1);
  uBit.io.P0.setDigitalValue(0);
 }
 release_fiber();
}
```

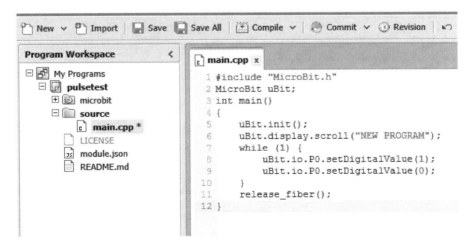

14

Compile the project, download the program and if you connect a logic analyzer or oscilloscope to P0 you will see the fastest pulse that the micro:bit can produce.

So programming in C/C++ gives you a 3.5 microsecond pulse or a 133kHz square wave. There is also a 0.1ms pause every 6ms, probably the system timer interrupting as the documentation gives the granularity of the system timer as 6ms. This should be compared with the same program in MicroPython that produces a 72 microsecond pulse, i.e around 20 times slower.

Is it possible to do better than 3.5 microseconds? Yes it is. As will be explained in Chapter 4, by using direct access to the hardware we can reduce the pulse width to about 0.5 microseconds.

Finally if you want a standard "blinky" test program, which as mentioned is the real hello world of mbed programming, try:

```
while(1)
{
 uBit.display.image.setPixelValue(2,2,255);
 uBit.sleep(100);
 uBit.display.image.setPixelValue(2,2,0);
 uBit.sleep(100);
}
```

The display function makes use of the display buffer implemented by the micro:bit library. There are ways of getting at the raw LEDs without using the display buffer but this is slightly more complicated.

You now know how to create and run a C/C++ program for the micro:bit.

At this point you could start to code anything you want. If you want to work offline however then you will need to do a little more work. Exactly how to work off line and how to use NetBeans as your development environment is described next.

# Chapter 2

# Offline C/C++ Development

Now we have discovered how to use the online editor to create a C/C++ program, we are going to move to the desktop with an offline approach. This has the advantage that we can use any tools we care to select and no Internet connection is needed.

Getting micro:bit development setup on the desktop isn't exactly the same as getting for general mbed development, but it very nearly is. The only real difference is the library used to support the hardware. To work locally we need to install the mbed build system which is called yotta, a suitable compiler tool set, and something to use as an editor. Fortunately this is all surprisingly easy once you know how.

## Build systems

The biggest problem facing the embedded programmer is the apparent complexity of the build system. Back in simpler times an embedded C program might grow to a few hundred lines, perhaps with a simple single support library. Today libraries such as mbed or the microbit library are complex and need other software components to complete them. You could manage these manually, which is what we did in the past. Each time you included a header you would have to find and resolve references to other headers and then find the object files corresponding to all of these libraries and link them into the final program. When the total amount of code was small this was entirely possible but, as already mentioned, this is no longer the case.

The solution to the problem is a build system which can do the job for you automatically. You may already know build tools such as **make** that run scripts that invoke the compiler and linker on all of the necessary files. A build system goes beyond this in that it will also deduce dependencies, perhaps even get the files needed, and incorporate them into the build. An example of such as system is **cmake** which generates make files for you.

For the mbed project a new build system called **yotta** was invented and it is currently under development. Offline development without using yotta is possible, but it would require you to manually organize all of the files needed to build the project and create the commands for the compiler and linker to perform the build; yotta can do this for you.

In fact yotta generates cmake files which are then used to build the system using make or **ninja**, which is the default build engine.

There are some problems with this approach. The first is that yotta is a complicated system and if things go wrong you can be left wondering what to do. Complex systems like yotta are great when they work, but quickly become a nightmare and a time waste when the don't. The second problem is that this is something new to learn. There are enough problems in embedded programming without adding another layer of complexity and, of course, the need to learn something new feeds back into the difficulties of working out what is going wrong. However in practice yotta turns out to be easy to use and mostly reliable.

## How yotta works

You don't need to know how yotta works under the covers to use it, but a little knowledge is helpful.

Yotta works with modules which roughly speaking is a group of code and header files that does something. A yotta module includes a json format file which provides metadata such as its name, license, author and any modules that it makes use of, i.e. its dependencies. You don't have to create the json file manually yotta has commands that do it for you.

Yotta also supports the same system for an executable and when you tell yotta to build the executable it reads the json file, gets the modules which are needed and then creates cmake files to build those modules for a specified platform - the target. Finally cmake generates files that are actually used to build the entire project using ninja or one of other make systems that it supports.

This is complicated because you have yotta feeding cmake, which feeds ninja, which does the final job of compiling and linking the code. If you are feeling confused it will make a lot more sense after you have seen yotta in action. Notice that as well as automating the build of your program you can also use yotta to create and publish modules that can then be used by other people.

## Installing yotta

Detailed instructions for installing yotta are provided on the mbed website

**http://yottadocs.mbed.com/**

Windows users should simply download latest yotta windows installer from the supplied link and run it. It enables you to pick all the components you need including **python**, which is what yotta is written in; **gcc** ,the gcc ARM cross compiler which you need to compile programs for the micro:bit; **cMake** needed to generate make/ninja files; **ninja**, which actually runs the compiler to generate the program and **yotta** itself.

18

A typical selection of options can be seen below:

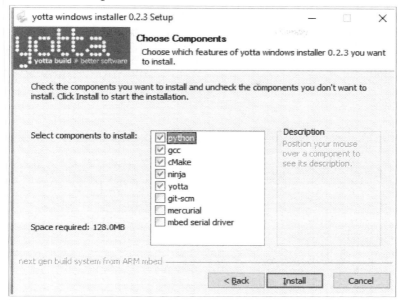

If you want to use either of the **git-scm** or **mercurial** version control programs then install these as well. The **mbed serial driver** will let you establish a serial connection to the micro:bit for debugging and other uses. If you don't already have it installed it is worth adding to the list.

The installer just gets on with the job and when it finishes you should be able to use yotta.

For OSX you can simply download and drag the yotta app:

**OS X yotta.app**

into the applications folder. When you run it a terminal will open.

Under Linux there is no installer, but it is easy to set things up using the package manager. You need to install the latest Python 2 - which is usually installed by default. You also need the latest **python-setuptools**, **cmake**, **ninja** and **pip**. You can then use pip to install **yotta**. You also need to install the ARM cross-compiler **gcc-arm-none-eabi**. On Ubuntu you need **gcc-arm-embedded** instead.

Before we move on there is one more dependency that is needed for the micro:bit. The compiled binary is converted to a hex format file suitable for flashing the micro:bit's memory. This needs a utility called **srecord**. This you can get from Sourceforge as a source file that you can build yourself.

Alternatively, and more simply, you can download a binary for Windows from:

**https://sourceforge.net/projects/srecord/files/srecord-win32/**

Simply **unzip srec_cat.exe** into the yotta directory.

If you don't do this then yotta will complain that it can't find srec_cat.exe in the final stage of the build and you will not have a .hex file in the output directory. Notice that while the micro:bit needs srecord, other mbed project targets don't.

## Creating a micro:bit project

You don't need to know all of the yotta commands to create and work with a micro:bit project. All you need to do is open a command prompt and move to the yotta installation directory, usually **c:/yotta** on Windows and run the batch file **run_yotta**. This sets the paths correctly to find all of the programs involved in using yotta. Alternatively you can run yotta via the icon that should have been installed on your desktop.

To create a new project you first create a new project directory and while in the directory use the command:

```
yotta init
```

For example, under Windows:

```
mkdir pulse cd pulse yotta init
```

At this point you will be asked a set of questions:

1.  Name of module - defaults to name of directory

2.  Initial version - defaults to 0.0.0

3.  Is this an executable? - Yes in this case, defaults to No

4.  short description - whatever you want to put

5.  Author - whatever you want to put

6.  License - your preferred license you want, defaults to Apache 2.0

Yotta creates a set of folders complete with a json file describing the project:

```
Name

    source
    test
    module.json
```

At this point the source and test folders are empty. These are where you are supposed to put your code files for the project and any tests you want to implement.

## Adding a dependency on the microbit library

You could start populating the source folder with whatever program you wanted to write, but a micro:bit program has a dependency on the microbit library which needs to be added. How this is done is slightly different from installing a standard mbed dependency.

At the moment the microbit library isn't hosted by mbed and so you have to download it from its GitHub repository. However, before we can add any dependencies we have to set the target for the project. In principle you only have to do this once for any yotta session, but in practice you might find that it gets forgotten or overwritten. For the micro:bit you set the target using:

```
yotta target bbc-microbit-classic-gcc
```

This adds a yotta_targets directory with some files that are needed for the target:

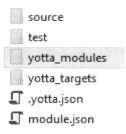

After this you can add the dependency on the microbit library:

```
yotta install lancaster-university/microbit
```

This might take a few minutes because the library is downloaded from GitHub.

After it is complete you will see a module folder has been added to the project.

This folder contains code for the libraries you will want to use in your programs:

ble
ble-nrf51822
mbed-classic
microbit
microbit-dal
nrf51-sdk

At this point you can build the project. If you plan to stay with yotta and use a simple editor to create your C/C++ files then this is how you will build your application each time.

If you plan to move to an IDE such as NetBeans then the IDE will make use of the ninja files created to build your program in the future.

So we just need to use yotta to build the project. The problem is that there are no files in the source or test folders and yotta will simply ignore any empty folders in the build. To give the system something to build we need to add a .cpp file in the source folder.

Use any editor to add something trivial like:

```
#include "MicroBit.h" MicroBit uBit; int main() {
uBit.init();
uBit.display.scroll("NEW PROGRAM");
release_fiber();
}
```

and store the result as **main.cpp** or any name you care to use.

Now we can build and test the program using:

```
yotta build
```

If you watch what happens you will see the program build and it will tell you that the build files have been written to the  build/bbc-microbit-classic-gcc directory int he project. The important part is that you will find the hex file in the directory:

```
pulse\build\bbc-microbit-classic-gcc\Source
```

The file that you need to download to the micro:bit is pulse-combined.hex and not the pulse.hex file. If you can't find a .hex file then check the messages produced by yotta and you will probably find that srec_cat.exe is mentioned as missing. See the instructions given earlier about obtaining and installing **srecord**.

If everything has worked you should see the "NEW PROGRAM" message scroll past.

This is all you need to do. You can now edit and add .cpp files to the source directory. If you need to add other dependencies then use the install command. Each time you use the build command new cmake and ninja files are generated so you can keep things up-to-date but also note that there is no point in editing any of the cmake or ninja files.

### Summary of project creation

1. Create a new folder and make it the current directory.

2. To create the project folders and basic files use:
   ```
   yotta init
   ```

3. To target a project for the micro:bit use:
   ```
   yotta target bbc-microbit-classic-gcc
   ```

4. To install the essential dependencies to run your new project use:
   ```
   yotta install lancaster-university/microbit
   ```

5. To install any other dependencies use the same command but change the name of the module or GitHub project you want to include.

6. Add at least one .cpp file to the source folder and to the test folder if you want to construct tests.

7. To build the project use:
   ```
   yotta build
   ```

8. The hex file you need to download will be found in:
   `project folder\build\bbc-microbit-classic-gcc\Source`
   and will be called
   `project-folder-combined.hex`

## Using NetBeans

While you can use the yotta route to building your programs, it is fairly easy to use an IDE such as NetBeans or Eclipse to make your job easier. The description here is for NetBeans, but getting Eclipse to work follows the same route.

It is assumed that you have yotta installed and working and have built a micro:bit program using yotta. You do not have to run it, unless you want to check that everything is working, just built it and have it ready to run.

It is also assumed that you have NetBeans for C/C++ projects installed and working.

You need to add the yotta directory to the path so that it can be found automatically by the build process.

In the case of Windows add **c:\yotta** to the existing path.

## Install make

If you are working with Windows you also need to download and install a version of make that works under Windows. You can get this by installing cygwin or mwin but the simplest way is to download **GNU make for Windows** from:

**http://gnuwin32.sourceforge.net/packages/make.htm**

Simply install it using the setup program and the default settings.

## Set up Tool Collection

Your first task in configuring NetBeans is to set up the tool collection. The ARM cross compilers that you need should be already set up as part of the yotta installation. To specify where they are you need to run NetBeans and use the command **Tools,Servers**.

If this is a new installation of NetBeans and you haven't created any C++ projects yet then the Server window might take some time to list C/C++ Build Hosts - wait for a few minutes.

Navigate down to C/C++ Build Hosts and expand the localhost node. Right click on ToolCollections under localhost and select add New Tool Collection.

In the dialog box that appears set the base directory to:

        `C:\yotta\gcc\bin`

This is where the compilers are stored, but NetBeans probably won't recognize them. We could create a new tool set definition but it is easier just to ignore the warning and press on. To unlock the dialog you need to select one of the other compiler set types, say cygwin, and then set it back to unknown and you will find you can enter a name for the tool set.

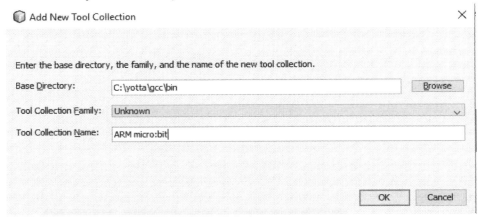

You now have to fill in the details of where to find the compilers etc manually as NetBeans does not automatically locate them:

### C Compiler

    C:\yotta\gcc\bin\arm-none-eabi-cpp.exe

### C++ Compiler

    C:\yotta\gcc\bin\arm-none-eabi-g++.exe

### Assembler

    C:\yotta\gcc\bin\arm-none-eabi-as.exe

### make

    C:\Program Files (x86)\GnuWin32\bin\make.exe

### Debugger

    C:\yotta\gcc\bin\arm-none-eabi-gdb.exe

Not all of these are required and you might have to change the directories depending on where things were installed.

The final step is to make sure that **c:\yotta** is in the path, even if other yotta directories are already there. To do this right click on **This PC**, select properties and select **Advanced system settings**. In the dialog box that appears click the **Environment Variables** button, edit **Path** in the **System Variables** list and add **c:\yotta;** to the start.

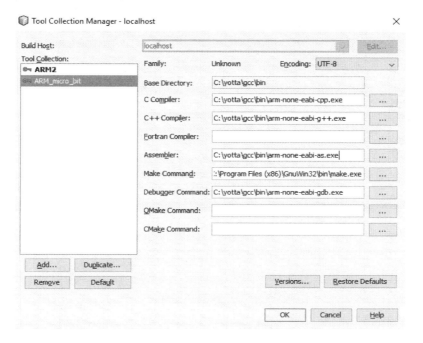

## Import the Project

With the tool collection specified we can now import the project we created using yotta. Simply use the command **File,New Project** and select **Project With Existing Sources**:

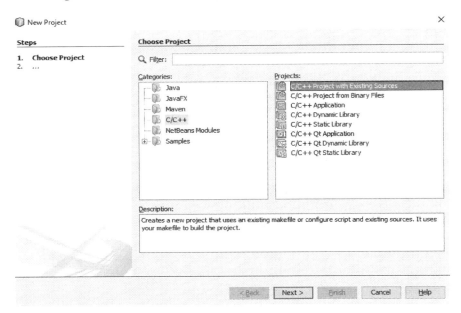

Finally navigate to the project directory:

    \build\bbc-microbit-classic-gcc

and import the project. It takes time for the project to import, but when it has you can try to build it.

In many cases you will see the message:

```
ninja: no work to do
```

because all of the files are up-to-date following the clean rebuild NetBeans has just performed.

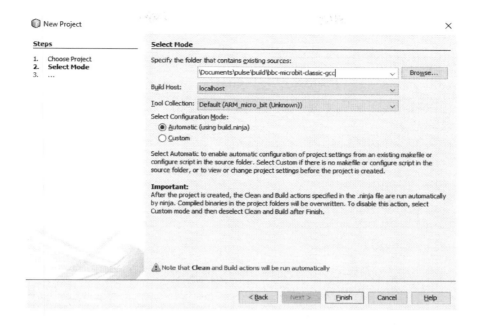

To give it a good test you need to edit the C++ source file and then rebuild. Alternatively you could try another full clean build but this will recompile the library so it is slow.

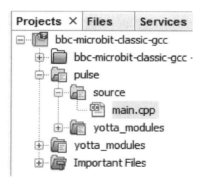

If you get an error message to the effect that ninja.exe cannot be found then you are missing c:\yotta in the path and you need to add it as described earlier. If you change the path variable you will need to restart NetBeans for it to have any effect.

You can now edit the source file and add files to the project and in most cases the build will compile the changes.

Notice that you cannot use the Run command as NetBeans has no idea how to run the file that it compiles. You need to use the Build or Clean Build commands - the "hammer" icons next to the green run icon.

You will find the hex file that has to be downloaded to the micro:bit in the usual directory:

```
project folder\build\bbc-microbit-classic-gcc\Source
```

and it will be called:

```
project-folder-combined.hex
```

So in this case the directory is:

```
pulse\build\bbc-microbit-classic-gcc\Source
```

and the file is called:

```
pulse-combined.hex
```

If you need to add another dependency or make structural changes to the project then you need to return to using yotta to modify things.

You usually have to build the project using yotta once before NetBeans notices the difference. The reason for this is that the changes are only put into the ninja files as part of a yotta build and NetBeans uses these to build your project.

The fact of the matter is that yotta is in charge of the project and NetBeans follows what it says.

From here you can explore other configurations and even automatic running of the project and debugging.

The most basic task when working with the micro:bit is controlling the I/O lines. This isn't difficult if you use the framework provided but there some subtle points to watch out for.

The micro:bit has 32 General Purpose I/O (GPIO) lines, although not all of them are available for use. Finding out how to use them is an important first step and you have to master both the hardware and the software aspects.

**Warning**

**Despite the ease of making connections to the micro:bit using ad-hoc cables and clips, the GPIO lines are very low power and sensitive to voltages and currents outside of their normal range.**

**Do not connect anything to the micro:bit, especially for output, without considering the voltage and current applied to the GPIO line.**

**The voltage should always be 3.3V or less and the current should be 0.5mA or less.**

## Pinouts

The big irritation with working with any electronic device that has GPIO lines is what do you call them. The manufacturer will have given them names like GPIO 01, GPIO 02 and so on, but when the processor is used in a finished product like the micro:bit these lines are brought out to physical pins or connections on the printed circuit board. These are then often called Pin01, Pin02 and so on and there is no need for Pin01 to correspond to GPIO 01, and indeed in most cases pin numbers and GPIO numbers are fairly independent.

Why does this matter?

The main reason is that the low level documentation provided by the chip manufacturer generally uses GPIO numbers and the documentation provided by the device manufacturer generally uses Pin numbers. You can see the potential for confusion and mistakes.

The framework functions all expect you to specify the GPIO number of the line you want to use but provide constants that map Pin number to GPIO number.

The definition of the constants can be found in MicroBitPin.h and as you can see there is no numerical logic in the assignments, even more so when you remember that the pins on the micro:bit's edge connector are not sequential!

| Pin | GPIO |
| --- | --- |
| MICROBIT_PIN_P0 | P0_3 |
| MICROBIT_PIN_P1 | P0_2 |
| MICROBIT_PIN_P2 | P0_1 |
| MICROBIT_PIN_P3 | P0_4 |
| MICROBIT_PIN_P4 | P0_5 |
| MICROBIT_PIN_P5 | P0_17 |
| MICROBIT_PIN_P6 | P0_12 |
| MICROBIT_PIN_P7 | P0_11 |
| MICROBIT_PIN_P8 | P0_18 |
| MICROBIT_PIN_P9 | P0_10 |
| MICROBIT_PIN_P10 | P0_6 |
| MICROBIT_PIN_P11 | P0_26 |
| MICROBIT_PIN_P12 | P0_20 |
| MICROBIT_PIN_P13 | P0_23 |
| MICROBIT_PIN_P14 | P0_22 |
| MICROBIT_PIN_P15 | P0_21 |
| MICROBIT_PIN_P16 | P0_16 |
| MICROBIT_PIN_P19 | P0_0 |
| MICROBIT_PIN_P20 | P0_30 |

The P0_n constants are the actual GPIO numbers and these are defined in PinNames.h as an enumeration with P0_0=0, P0_1=1 and so on. This would be the end of the story if it wasn't for the fact that some of the GPIO lines are used for specific jobs within the micro:bit.

As you can see  in the standard pinout diagram, most of the GPIO lines already have jobs. If you want to use them for your own purposes then what ever they are doing for the micro:bit has to be turned off. For example if you use any of the GPIO lines that are assigned to the LED display then you cannot use the LED display and if you do then this will take over the GPIO lines that you are nominally using.

The only GPIO lines that are completely free to use are:

**Free GPOIO Pins**
MICROBIT_PIN_P0
MICROBIT_PIN_P1
MICROBIT_PIN_P2
MICROBIT_PIN_P8
MICROBIT_PIN_P16

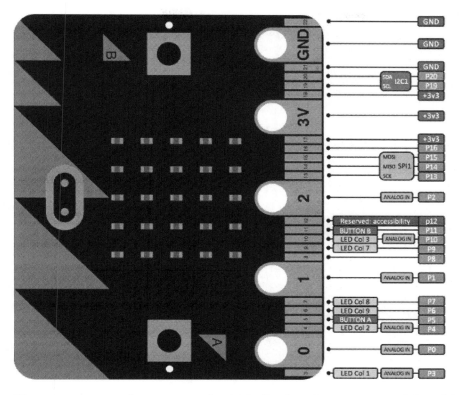

If you are prepared not to use the LED display then you can add to this list:

**LED Display Pins**
```
MICROBIT_PIN_P3
MICROBIT_PIN_P4
MICROBIT_PIN_P6
MICROBIT_PIN_P7
MICROBIT_PIN_P9
MICROBIT_PIN_P10
```

If you are prepared not to use Button A and B you can add:

**Button Pins**
```
MICROBIT_PIN_P5
MICROBIT_PIN_P11
```

In most cases you probably don't want to make use of the SPI bus so you can to the list:

**SPI Bus Pins**
```
MICROBIT_PIN_P13
MICROBIT_PIN_P14
MICROBIT_PIN_P15
```

Finally we have three pins dedicated to the I2C bus which you can use, but you need to know that these are connected to the accelerometer and magnetometer which you can use if you take them over. Notice that you can use them for your devices on the I2C bus without disabling the on board devices:

**I2C Bus Pins**
```
MICROBIT_PIN_P19
MICROBIT_PIN_P20
```

There are also some GPIO lines used internally and not brought out onto the edge connector. For example as well as six pins on the edge connector the LED display makes  use of:

**LED MATRIX COLS**
```
    COL1 = p4
    COL2 = p5
    COL3 = p6
    COL4 = p7
    COL5 = p8
    COL6 = p9
    COL7 = p10
    COL8 = p11
    COL9 = p12
```
**LED MATRIX ROWS**
```
    ROW1 = p13
    ROW2 = p14
    ROW3 = p15
```

The USB serial interface uses:

**RX AND TX PINS**
```
    TGT_TX = p24
    TGT_RX = p25
```

Finally three GPIO lines are used as interrupt lines from the accelerometer and magnetometer:

```
ACCEL INTERRUPT PINS (MMA8653FC)
    ACCEL_INT2 = p27
    ACCEL_INT1 = p28
MAGNETOMETER INTERRUPT PIN (MAG3110)
    MAG_INT1 = p29
```

Notice that while you can't use any of these internal GPIO lines for your own devices knowing what they control can still be useful.

## GPIO Capabilities

Another complication is that GPIO lines can be assigned to other internal devices within the processor. For example, the serial hardware (UART) can make use of any two GPIO lines for its RX and TX pins.

There is also a single AtoD converter device and this can be connected to any of a subset of GPIO lines that then act as analog inputs. To create analog outputs, the Pulse Width Modulation (PWM) capabilities of some of the GPIO lines is used - see Chapter 5. By pairing the AtoD with the DtoA provided by the PWM some of the pins are designated as analog capable.

**Analog GPIO Pins**
```
MICROBIT_PIN_P0
MICROBIT_PIN_P1
MICROBIT_PIN_P2
MICROBIT_PIN_P3
MICROBIT_PIN_P4
MICROBIT_PIN_P10
```

Notice that pins 3, 4 and 10 are involved in driving the LED display and this allows for some interesting possibilities such as using the array as a light sensor.

In the case of the micro:bit there is also a GPIO mode that allows you to use the pin as a debounced high impedance input on pins P0, P1 and P2. This makes it easy to use things like fruit and other objects as creative input devices.

## Digital GPIO

With all of these possibilities, using the GPIO lines can seem quite complicated. For simplicity, and because it is the most common way they are used, we will concentrate on their use as simple digital I/O lines and, for the moment, ignore analog, PWM and touch outputs and their use as I2C and SPI buses all of which are covered in later chapters.

The basic interface to the GPIO lines is the MicroBitPin object. You can create and use MicroBitPin objects as needed or you can use the MicroBitPin objects created on the uBit object. If you create your own MicroBitPin objects create them as global objects and do not create a uBit object.

For example, to access Pin 0 you can either use:

```
#include "MicroBit.h"
MicroBit uBit;
main(){
    uBit.init();
    uBit.io.P0.setDigitalValue(1);
}
```

or

```
#include "MicroBit.h"
main(){
 MicroBitPin P0(MICROBIT_ID_IO_P0, MICROBIT_PIN_P0,
PIN_CAPABILITY_ALL);
 P0.setDigitalValue(1);
}
```

Don't worry about the MicroBitPin constructor or the setDigitalValue function. All that matters at the moment is that you see the two ways of getting at a GPIO line.

If you are not troubled by resource shortages use the uBit object approach because it frees you from having to instantiate a MicroBitPin object for each pin. If you are having resource problems then instantiating only the objects you are going to use is a better strategy.

Notice that when you work with the uBit object the GPIO lines are just referred to as P0, P1 and so on. When you work with the MicroBitPin object directly the lines are referred to as MICROBIT_PIN_P0 etc. Be careful not to confuse the two naming systems.

If you want to create MicroBitPin objects then the constructor allows you to specify an event id, pin name and pin capability, i.e. what you are going to use the pin for.

```
MicroBitPin(int id,PinName name, PinCapability capability)
```

In most cases you use the message bus id provided for you. PinCapability is one of:

```
PIN_CAPABILITY_DIGITAL
PIN_CAPABILITY_ANALOG
PIN_CAPABILITY_AD
PIN_CAPABILITY_ALL
```

Compared to other GPIO libraries the strangest thing about the micro:bit's framework is that it doesn't have functions that set the direction of a GPIO line. Instead the direction is set the first time you try to read or write a line. To write a 0 or a 1 to the line you would use:

```
int setDigitalValue(int value)
```

and to read a line:

```
int getDigitalValue()
```

This approach has the advantage of not needing much in the way of initialization but if the line isn't already set up correctly for reading or writing then it takes extra time to configure it. What this means is that the first time you read or write a line it can take longer than the second and subsequent use. As a result it is sometimes necessary to do an extra read or write to the line before you start using it as a way of setting things up.

Apart from these two main function there are a few useful utilities. You can test to see if a GPIO line is currently a digital line and if it is an input or an output:

```
int isDigital()
int isInput()
int isOutput()
```

# Drive Type

The GPIO output can be configured into one of a number of modes but the most important is pull-up/down. Before we get to the code to do the job it is worth spending a moment explaining the three basic output modes, pushpull, pullup and pulldown.

## Pushpull Mode

In pushpull mode, which is the standard configuration for a GPIO output, two transistors of opposite polarity are used:

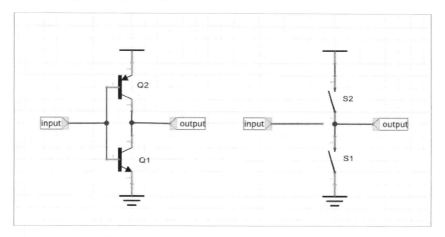

The circuit behaves like the two-switch equivalent shown on the right. Only one of the transistors, or switches, is "closed" at any time.

If the input is high then Q1 is saturated and the output is connected to ground - exactly as if S1 was closed. If the input is low then Q2 is saturated and it is as if S2 was closed and the output is connected to +V. You can see that this pushes the output line high with the same "force" as it pulls it low.

## Pullup Mode

In pullup mode one of the transistors is replaced by a resistor. It is used, for example, in a serial bus configuration like the I2C bus.

In this case the circuit is equivalent to having a single switch. When the switch is closed the output line is connected to ground and hence driven low. When the switch is open the output line is pulled high by the resistor.

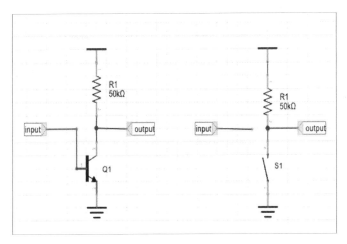

You can see that in this case the degree of pulldown is greater than the pullup, where the current is limited by the resistor. The advantage of this mode is that it can be used in an AND configuration. If multiple GPIO or other lines are connected to the output, then any one of them being low will pull the output line low. Only when all of them are off does the resistor succeed in pulling the line high.

## Pulldown Mode

Finally pulldown mode is exactly the same as the pullup only now the resistor is used to pull the output line low.

In the case of the pulldown mode the line is held high by the transistor but pulled low by the resistor only when all the switches are open. Putting this the other way round,- the line is high if any one switch is closed.

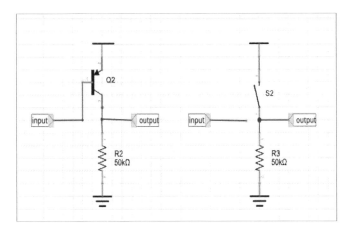

To set the mode for a GPIO line the function to use is:

```
int setPull ( PinMode pull)
```

where pull is any of:

```
PullUp
PullDown
PullNone
```

PullNone is the default and the value of the pull up/down resistor is in the range 10 to 16K. What this means is that in most cases you will probably have to add an external pull up/down resistor to bring the resistance down.

## GPIO Drive Characteristics

There is an important question to be answered - what can be safely connected to a GPIO line?

There is no problem connecting things to GPIO lines set to input, which is the default. The only thing you have to check is that the input doesn't go above 3.3V. If it does you could damage the GPIO line and the micro:bit.

When it comes to output you have to be much more cautious to avoid damage to the micro:bit. It is all a matter of how much current the line can source or sink. Obviously the output varies between 0V and 3.3V which is the working voltage of the micro:bit. So you can only connect devices which can operate at 3.3V, but there is also the issue of how much current the device needs to operate.

One of the most difficult specifications to find is how much current the GPIO lines will provide. The reason is partly that the situation is complicated. There are a number of ways that the GPIO line can be set up and there is a limit on the total current in all of the lines as well as a per-line limit.

What is very clear however is that the current handling ability of the micro:bit is very low. This is a problem because of the way that the GPIO lines are made very easy to access using clips and plugs makes it all too easy to connect a device directly to the line without thinking about the possibilities of damaging it. For example, you cannot safely conned an LED to the micro:bit - the current draw is simply too much.

In normal operation the GPIO lines are all configured into standard drive mode which limits the current to 0.5mA. This is a very small current. By comparison the Raspberry Pi can work with 3mA on each GPIO line and a single line can work up to 16mA.

There are high current drive modes which can be selected, as discussed the next chapter. With high current drive on a GPIO line can work with a maximum of 5mA, however the total current on all the GPIO pins cannot exceed 15mA. So you could have three GPIO lines drawing 5mA each or two drawing 5mA and five more drawing 1mA each. Notice also that you can set high current drive on a per line basis. That is one line can be high current drive and the next standard. Each line is subject to a 5mA or a 0.5mA maximum current according to its mode.

This is complicated, so a summary will help:

- In input mode you only have to keep the voltage on a GPIO line between 0 and 3.3V. The GPIO line in input mode is high impedance and draws little current from whatever is connected to it.

- In output mode with the default standard drive the voltage is between 0 and 3.3V and the current has to be less than 0.5mA

- In output mode a GPIO line with high drive turned on the current has to be less than 5mA.

- The total current in all of the GPIO lines has to be less than 15mA.

You cannot set high drive mode on using the framework. To do this you have to access the hardware directly, as detailed in the next chapter. In addition to setting the drive strength, you can also opt for open collector or open emitter.

The bottom line is that in nearly all cases if you want to drive something from a GPIO line you will need to use a transistor or a Field Effect Transistor (FET) to increase the current and perhaps change the voltage. If you have used an LED or other device from a GPIO line without a transistor or FET as a buffer and it worked, either you have been lucky or the drive specifications are pessimistic. However some users have destroyed their micro:bits doing this.

## An FET Buffer

Constructing a buffer is very easy and cheap. You can use a Bipolar Junction Transistor (BJT) if you want to, but in this case the simplest solution is to use an FET. The reason is that an FET hardly draws any current from the GPIO line.

Not only does the FET increase the current in the load it also allows you to change the drive voltage. Although the voltage in this circuit is shown as 3.3V it can be 5V or anything needed to drive the load. The FET isolates the micro:bit from the higher voltage.

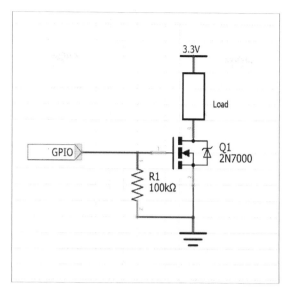

The 100K Ohm resistor is there to ensure that the FET and the load is off when the micro:bit first powers up and the GPIO line defaults to an input. Without it the FET would pick up noise and switch on and off randomly.

The FET shown, 2N7000, is cheap and can work with voltages up to 60V and currents up to 100mA. If you need a higher voltage or a larger current you will need to use a different FET. Power FETs are cheap, a few dollars, and can handle currents of tens of amps.

## GPIO Output

When you are generating GPIO output signals, the key questions are often when does the signal go high and when does it go low. In some applications this is a non-time critical event. As long as the line goes high or low in response to something then all is well. In other situations the response has to be after a given amount of time. If that time interval is longer than 100ms then there is generally no problem. If the interval is less than 100ms then you have to work out the best way to ensure the delay taking account of how accurate it has to be. Here we take a look at how fast GPIO lines can be changed and what sort of accuracy is possible.

### How Fast?

A fundamental question that you have to answer for any processor intended for use in embedded or IoT projects is how fast can the GPIO lines work?

Sometimes the answer isn't of too much concern because what you want to do only works relatively slowly. Any application that is happy with response times in the tens of millisecond region will generally work with almost any processor. However if you want to implement custom protocols or anything that needs microsecond responses the question is much more important.

It is fairly easy to find out how fast a single GPIO line can be used if you have a logic analyzer or oscilloscope. All you have to do is run the program that we used as a first test in Chapter 1:

```
uBit.init();
while(1) {
    uBit.io.P0.setDigitalValue(1);
    uBit.io.P0.setDigitalValue(0);
}
```

The results is a pulse train with pulses ranging from 3.5 to 3.8 microseconds and a 0.1ms pause every 6ms due to the system timer interrupting. There isn't anything that can be done about this 6ms interrupt apart from switching off the system timer.

## Delay Using Sleep

To generate pulses of a known duration we need to pause the program between state changes.

The simplest way of sleeping a fiber is to use the sleep command. Unfortunately this uses the system timer and only works in steps of 6ms.

To try this, include a call to sleep(9) to delay the pulse:

```
while(1) {
    uBit.io.P0.setDigitalValue(1);
    uBit.sleep(9);
    uBit.io.P0.setDigitalValue(0);
    uBit.sleep(9);
}
```

You will discover that you get 12ms pulses. This is only useful if you want pulses that are multiples of 6ms or so long that a 6ms error doesn't matter.

There is a microsecond delay function **wait_us()** which is part of the mbed software that the framework is built on and we can call it from a micro:bit program.

Unfortunately there is an overhead in calling the function. For example:

```
while(1) {
    uBit.io.P0.setDigitalValue(1);
    wait_us(20);
    uBit.io.P0.setDigitalValue(0);
    wait_us(20);
}
```

produces pulses that last just over 32 micro seconds.

If you look at how the delay time relates to the average pulse length things seem fairly simple and we have:

```
pulse length = delay+12
```

What this means is that if you want to set a delay less than 12 microseconds don't use wait_us. For delays bigger than this it works reasonably well. You can try various modifications to the basic wait_us approach but the best you can do is to get the overheads down to about 7 microseconds.

## Busy Wait

For pulses of less than about 50 microseconds it is better to use a busy wait, i.e. a loop that does nothing. You have to be a little careful about how you insert a loop that does nothing because optimizing compiler have a tendency to take a null loop out in an effort to make your program run faster. To stop an optimizing from removing busy wait loops make sure you always declare loop variables as volatile.

To generate a pulse of a given length you can use:

```
volatile int i;
    while (1) {
        for (i = 0; i < n; i++) {};
        uBit.io.P0.setDigitalValue(1);
        for (i = 0; i < n; i++) {};
        uBit.io.P0.setDigitalValue(0);
    }
```

where n is set to a value that depends on the delay you want to generate.

The relationship between n and t the time delay is linear:

```
n=1.333t - 5.83
```

and it means you can't generate pulses less than about 6 microseconds. For example, if you want pulses of around 10 microseconds, n=7 results in:

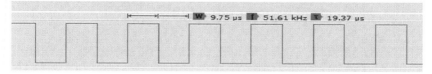

We will revisit the busy wait option and using timers in the next chapter.

## Phased Pulses

As a simple example of using the output functions let's try to write a short program that pulses two lines - one high and one low and then one low and one high' i.e. two pulse trains out of phase by 180 degrees.

The simplest program to do this job is:

```
while (1) {
        uBit.io.P0.setDigitalValue(1);
        uBit.io.P1.setDigitalValue(0);
        uBit.io.P0.setDigitalValue(0);
        uBit.io.P1.setDigitalValue(1);
    }
```

Notice that there is no delay in the loop so the pulses are produced at the fastest possible speed.

Using a logic analyzer reveals that the result isn't what you might expect:

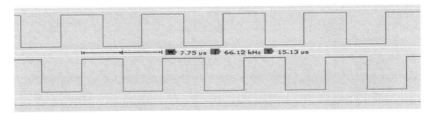

You can also see that the pulse trains are not 180 degrees out of phase. The top train switches on and the bottom train takes about half a pulse before it switches on, whereas the intent is for both actions to occur at the same time. You should also notice that now the pulse time is about 7.75 microseconds which is about double the time for a pulse train on a single GPIO line. The point is that it does take quite a long time to access and change the state of an output line.

Of course if we include a delay to increase the pulse width then the delay caused by accessing the GPIO lines in two separate actions isn't so obvious:

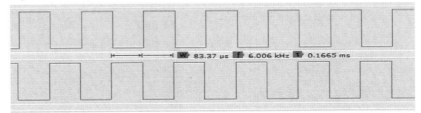

In this case the loop now has n=100:

```
volatile int i;
    while (1) {
        for (i = 0; i < 100; i++) {};
        uBit.io.P0.setDigitalValue(1);
        uBit.io.P1.setDigitalValue(0);
        for (i = 0; i < 100; i++) {};
        uBit.io.P0.setDigitalValue(0);
        uBit.io.P1.setDigitalValue(1);
    }
```

You will notice that the pulses are now roughly 80 microseconds wide and they are changing at what looks like nearer to being the same time - of course they aren't.

There is still a lag, but in many applications it might not be important. In other applications it could be crucial.

For example, if the two pulse trains were driving different halves of a motor controller bridge there would be a significant time when both were high - so shorting the power supply. It might only be for 10 microseconds but over time it could well damage the power supply. Of course, any sensible, cautious, engineer wouldn't feed a motor control bridge from two independently generated pulse trains unless they were guaranteed not to switch both sides of the bridge on at the same time.

A better way to generate multiple pulses is to write directly to the hardware, which is what we do in the next chapter.

### Summary of creating accurate pulses

- For delays greater than 6ms to an accuracy of 6ms use sleep().
- For delays from around 12 microseconds use wait_us which is accurate to around 1 microsecond.
- For delays greater than 7 microseconds use a busy wait which is accurate to around 1 microsecond.
- Switching GPIO lines takes time and achieving synchronized switching better than 10 microseconds is not possible using the framework.

## GPIO Input

GPIO input can be a much more difficult problem than output. At least for output you can see the change in the signal on a logic analyzer and know the exact time that it occurred. This makes if possible to track down timing problems and fine tune things with good accuracy.

Input on the other hand is "silent" and unobservable. When did you read in the status of the line? Usually the timing of the read is with respect to some other action that the micro:bit has taken. For example, input line 20 is read a given number of microseconds after setting the output line high. The usual rule of thumb is to assume that it takes as long to read a GPIO line as it does to set it. This means we can use the delay mechanisms that we looked at with output in mind for input. In some applications the times are long and/or unimportant but in some they are critical.

## Basic Input Circuit - The Switch

One of the most common input circuits is the switch or button and the micro:bit already has two built-in buttons, A and B. If you want another, external, button you can use any GPIO line and the following circuit:

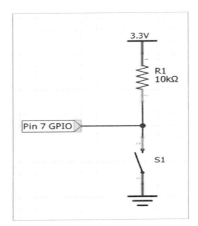

The 10K resistor isn't critical in value. It simply pulls the GPIO line high when the switch isn't pressed. When it is pressed a current of a little more than 0.3mA flows in the resistor. If this is too much, increase the resistance to 100K or even more, but notice that the higher the resistor value the noisier the input to the GPIO and the more it is susceptible to RF interference.

If you want a switch that pulls the line high instead of low, to reverse the logic just swap the positions of the resistor and the switch in the diagram.

Although the switch is the simplest input device, it is also very difficult to get right. When a user clicks a switch of any sort the action isn't clean - the switch bounces. What this means is that the logic level on the GPIO line goes high then low and high and bounces between the two until it settles down.

There are electronic ways of debouncing switches but software does the job much better. All you have to do is put a delay of a millisecond or so after detecting a switch press and read the line again. If it is still low then record a switch press. Similarly when the switch is released read the state twice with a delay. You can vary the delay to modify the perceived characteristics of the switch.

# The Potential Divider

If you have an input that is outside the range of 0 to 3.3V, you can reduce it using a simple potential divider. V is the input from the external logic and Vout it the connection to the GPIO input line:

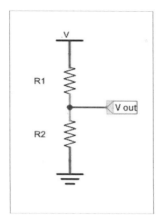

You can spend a lot of time on working out good values of R1 and R2. For loads that take a lot of current you need R1+R2 to be small and divided in the same ratio as the voltages. For example, for a 5V device R1=18K and R2=33K work well to drop the voltage to 3.3V.

The problem with a resistive divider is that it can round off fast pulses due to the small capacitive effects. This usually isn't a problem, but if it is then the solution is to use an FET buffer again.

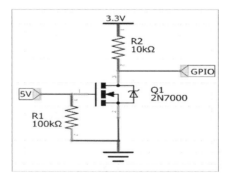

Notice that this is an inverting buffer, but you can usually ignore this and simply correct by inverting in software, i.e. read a 1 as a low and a 0 as a high state. The role of R1 is to make sure the FET is off when the 5V signal is absent and R2 limits the current in the FET to about 0.3mA. In most case you should try the simple voltage divider and only move to an active buffer if it doesn't work.

# How Fast Can We Measure?

The simplest way to find out how quickly we can take a measurement using the micro:bit is to perform a pulse width measurement using a busy wait. Applying a square wave to P0 we can measure the time that the pulse is high:

```
uBit.init();
uint32_t start;
volatile int i;
while (1) {
    while(1== uBit.io.P0.getDigitalValue());
    while(0== uBit.io.P0.getDigitalValue());
    for(i=0;i<1000;i++){
     if(0==uBit.io.P0.getDigitalValue()) break;
    }
    printf("%d\n\r",i);
}
```

This might look a little strange at first. The inner while loops are responsible for getting us to the right point in the waveform. First we loop until the line goes low, then we loop until it goes high again, and finally we measure how long before it goes low. You might think that we simply have to wait for it to go high and then measure how long till it goes low, but this misses the possibility that the signal might be part way through a high period when we first measure it.

If you run this program with different pulse widths the result are very regular:

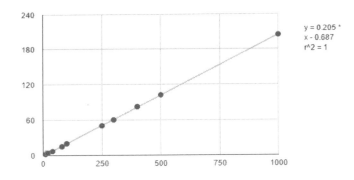

In the chart loop count is on the y-axis, pulse time on the x-axis.

The equation relating time t and loop count n is:

```
t=4.88 n +3.38 microseconds
```

This works down to about 10 microseconds or slightly less.

If you want to record the time in microseconds, rather than using a loop count you could use:

```
uBit.init();
uint32_t t;
volatile int i;
while (1) {
     while(1== uBit.io.P0.getDigitalValue());
     while(0== uBit.io.P0.getDigitalValue());
     t = us_ticker_read();
     for(i=0;i<1000;i++){
      if(0==uBit.io.P0.getDigitalValue()) break;
     }
     t= us_ticker_read()-t;
     printf("%d,%ld\n\r",i,t);
}
```

This is accurate to around 10 microseconds.

In either case, if you try measuring pulse widths much shorter than the lower limit that works, you will get results that look as if longer pulses are being applied. The reason is simply that the micro:bit will miss the first transition to zero but will detect a second or third or later transition. This is the digital equivalent of the aliasing effect found in the Fourier Transform or general signal processing.

## Interrupts

There is a general feeling that realtime programming and interrupts go together and if you are not using an interrupt you are probably doing something wrong. In fact, if you are using an interrupt you probably are doing something wrong. Some organizations agree with the general idea that interrupts are dangerous to the extent they ban them being used at all, and this includes realtime software.

In the case of the micro:bit we have a system of events that stand in as a software wrapping of the raw system interrupts that are available if you dig just a little deeper.

As far as GPIO lines are concerned you can set determine how event to occur using one of four settings. The most commonly useful is the on-edge setting which fires an event if a GPIO line transitions from high to low or low to high.

You can set the event type using the command:

```
int eventOn(int eventType)
```

where eventType is one of:

| | |
|---|---|
| MICROBIT_PIN_EVENT_ON_EDGE | Fire on rising or falling edge as specified when event registered |
| MICROBIT_PIN_EVENT_ON_PULSE | Fire if pin is high or low as set when event registered |
| MICROBIT_PIN_EVENT_ON_TOUCH | Fire if pin touched |
| MICROBIT_PIN_EVENT_NONE | Disable events for this pin |

As well as the eventOn setting you also have to register the event with the messagebus. You have to supply the, id of the pin generating the event, the event type, the function to be called when the event happens and how the event should be handled.

For example:

```
bus.listen(MICROBIT_ID_IO_P0, MICROBIT_PIN_EVT_PULSE_HI,
              onPulse, MESSAGE_BUS_LISTENER_IMMEDIATE)
```

will call onPulse when the PULSE HI event occurs on pin P0 and it will call the event handler at once. The event types that you can specify are:

```
MICROBIT_PIN_EVT_RISE
MICROBIT_PIN_EVT_FALL
MICROBIT_PIN_EVT_PULSE_HI
MICROBIT_PIN_EVT_PULSE_LO
```

The event handler has the signature:

```
void eventHandler(MicroBitEvent evt)
```

and one of the most useful properties of the evt object is the timestamp of the event.

Events are only really useful when you have a low frequency condition that needs to be dealt with on a low priority basis. Their use can simplify the logic of your program, but rarely does using an event speed things up because the overhead involved in event or interrupt handling is usually quite high.

For example, suppose you want to react to a doorbell push button. You could write a polling loop that simply checks the button status repeatedly and forever, or you could write an event to respond to the doorbell. How good a design this is depends on how much the doorbell press event has to interact with the rest of the program.

Finally, before you dismiss the idea of having a micro:bit do nothing but ask repeatedly "is the doorbell pressed", consider what else it has to do. If it is "not much" then a polling loop might well be your simplest option.

Let's find out how much overhead is inherent in using events by repeating the pulse width measurement. This time we can't simply print the results as this would stop the event handling. As a compromise we save 20 readings in an array and then print them.

It is also important to keep the event handling routines short as how long they take to complete. If the event handling routine takes longer then the pulse width that can be measured is longer.

```
uint64_t t[20];
uint64_t temp=0;
int i=0;
 void onPulseEdge(MicroBitEvent evt)
 {
  t[i]=(evt.timestamp-temp);
  i++;
  temp = evt.timestamp;
    if(i<20)return;
    uBit.io.P0.eventOn(MICROBIT_PIN_EVENT_NONE);
    for(i=1;i<20;i++){
        printf("%d\n\r",(int)t[i]);
    }
 }

int main() {
    uBit.init();
    uBit.messageBus.listen(MICROBIT_ID_IO_P0,
                    MICROBIT_PIN_EVT_RISE ,
                    onPulseEdge,
                    MESSAGE_BUS_LISTENER_IMMEDIATE) ;
    uBit.messageBus.listen(MICROBIT_ID_IO_P0,
                    MICROBIT_PIN_EVT_FALL ,
                    onPulseEdge,
                    MESSAGE_BUS_LISTENER_IMMEDIATE) ;
    uBit.io.P0.eventOn(MICROBIT_PIN_EVENT_ON_EDGE);
```

Notice we have the event handler called when there is a rising edge and a falling edge.

This records accurate times for pulses longer than 250 microseconds but starts to miss pulses as the pulse width shortens to 100 microseconds, when it misses about one pulse in ten. If the event handlers take longer to do their task then the limit would be even larger.

Events are great for handling things that happen on the scale of 100s of microseconds and preferably 1millisecond.

Also notice that the documentation says that the shortest pulse that can be reliably detected, i.e. will fire a MICROBIT_PIN_EVENT_ON_PULSE event, is 85 microseconds.

Events are only useful if the time that the event handler takes, plus the overheads of servicing an event is less than the average repetition rate of the event.

# Chapter 4

# Fast Memory Mapped GPIO

The framework makes working with the GPIO and other devices as easy as it can be, but there are many layers of software to go through before you get to the hardware. Writing directly to the hardware can make things up to ten times faster and give you access to things that their framework doesn't. It is also an educational experience to deal with the raw hardware directly.

All of the peripherals that are directly connected to the processor are memory mapped. What this means is that there are a set of addresses that correspond to "registers" that control and give the devices status. Using these is just a matter of knowing what addresses to use and the format of the registers.

This is easy to say, but can be difficult to get right, at least initially. After you have got it right you might forget what all the fuss was about.

The best way to understand how all of this works is to find out about a particular peripheral, the GPIO.

## The GPIO Registers

If you look at the manual for the RF51 series processor you will find a long section on the registers that are connected to the GPIO lines. This looks very complicated, but in fact it comes down to a very simple pattern.

There are 32 GPIO lines, not all usable on the micro:bit. For each GPIO line there is a single configuration register, i.e. 32 registers - one for each line.

There is also a single 32-bit OUT register that is used to set each output line to high or low with each bit corresponding to the state of one line; and a single 32-bit IN register used to read the state of all 32 GPIO lines with one bit per line.

In theory these are the only registers you need to know about to use the GPIO lines, but five more are provided to make things easier.

The OUTSET and OUTCLR registers can be used to set or clear any GPIO lines without changing the state of the others. If you write to either register then the lines that correspond to one bits are set or cleared according to which register you write to.

For example, suppose you want to set GPIO Pin0 to a one then you could write 0x01 to the OUT register. However, this sets all of the other 31 pins to zero. If you write 0x01 to the OUTSET register then you set Pin 0 high and leave all of the others in their current state. Similarly, writing 0x01 to OUTCLR sets Pin 0 low and leaves the other in their current state.

There is also a 32-bit DIR register which can be used to set any combination of pins to input or output depending on whether you write a zero or a one to the corresponding bit location.

DIRSET and DIRCLR register set the GPIO line either to output or input when you write a one to the corresponding bit location and make it easier for you to set lines to input or output without altering what the remaining lines are set to.

Writing 0x01 to DIR will set Pin 0 to output but all of the remaining 31 pins to input.

Writing 0x01 to DIRSET will set only Pin 0 to output and writing it to DIRCLR will set only Pin 0 to input.

To summarize, the registers controlling the GPIO lines are:

- 32 PIN_CNF[n] configuration registers, one for each GPIO line
- OUT  sets the any combination of GPIO lines high or low
  OUTSET sets any combination of GPIO lines high
  OUTCLR sets any combination of GPIO lines low
- IN reads the state of all GPIO lines
- DIR sets the I/O direction of any combination of GPIO lines
  DIRSET sets any combination of GPIO lines to output
  DIRCLR sets any combination of GPIO lines to input

Of course we need to know which bits in the configuration register controls what aspect of the GPIO line.

```
Bits
0        DIR    0=input 1=output
1        INPUT  0=disconnect input   1=connect input
3,2      PULL   00= No Pull, 01=Pull Down, 11=Pull Up
10,9,8 DRIVE 000 S0S1
             001 H0S1
             010 S0H1
             011 H0H1
             100 D0S1
             101 D0H1
             110 S0D1
             111 H0D1
17,16   SENSE 00=disabled, 01=High, 11= Low
```

We already know about DIR and PULL from the previous chapter and to understand DRIVE all you really need to know is that there are two possibilities for the pushpull transistor arrangement.

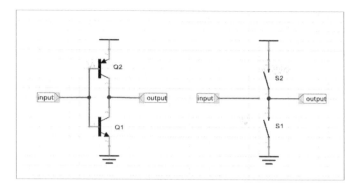

The two transistors can either be Standard drive, i.e. 0.5mA, or High drive, i.e. 5mA. The bottom transistor pulls the output low to give a zero and the top transistor pulls the output high to give a one. Hence a DRIVE, or S0H1, has a high drive for the top transistor and a standard drive for the bottom transistor. That is, the GPIO line can sink 0.5mA and supply 5mA to a load.

The D in the specification simply means Disconnected, i.e. there is no transistor in that position in the drive. So H0D1 has the pullup transistor missing, giving an open collector drive.

In most cases you either want S0S1 or H0H1 - the others are for special situations.

The INPUT bit simply disconnects the input buffer if you set it to one. The reasons for wanting to do this are to reduce the loading and decouple input from output.

The SENSE bits control when the pin will contribute to generating a DETECT signal. This is used to bring the processor out of power saving mode and in more complex ways to automatically trigger other actions. You can ignore this for the moment.

The only question we have to answer now is, where are the registers?

The GPIO registers occupy a block of memory starting at 0x50000000 and the register addresses are specified as offsets from this starting point in two blocks:

```
OUT          0x504
OUTSET       0x508
OUTCLR       0x50C
IN           0x510
DIR          0x514
DIRSET       0x518
DIRCLR       0x51C
PIN_CNF[n]   0x700 +4*n
```

# A Fast Pulse

Putting all this together we now only have the problem of how to implement it in a C program.

We can usually leave the GPIO line we want to use in its default configuration and simply set its direction and state. Notice that you do have to be careful not to modify the direction or state of any GPIO lines that are used internally by the micro:bit.

To set and clear a single line we just need access to three registers DIR, OUTSET and OUTCLR. We need to store the addresses of these registers in suitable pointers:

```
volatile unsigned int *dirset=(unsigned int *)(0x50000000UL+0x518);
volatile unsigned int *outset=(unsigned int *)(0x50000000UL+0x508);
volatile unsigned int *outclr=(unsigned int *)(0x50000000UL+0x50C);
```

The pointers need to be unsigned 32-bit integers and they are marked as volatile to make sure the compiler doesn't optimize away any repeated use of them.

Next all we need to do is create a mask that picks out the bit corresponding to the pin we want to toggle. You need to keep in mind that the bit at position b corresponds to the internal GPIO line numbering and not the physical pins on the micro:bit. For example, if you want to pulse Pin 0 on the micro:bit you need to pulse GPIO Pin 3. You can use the table in the previous chapter to look up edge connector pin names and find out which GPIO line is driving them.

GPIO Pin 3 corresponds to bit 3 in the register and in general we need to construct a bit "mask" that sets the bits corresponding to the GPIO lines we want to control. The easiest way to do this is to left shift a 0x1 to the correct location. That is, if you want to work with GPIO line Pin b you would create a mask using:

```
unsigned int b=0x01<<b;
```

So if we want to work with GPIO Pin 3 we need a mask:

```
unsigned int mask = 1 << 3;
```

You can construct masks for multiple pins by ORing together masks for multiple pins or by simply working out the hex value needed.

In our case for GPIO Pin 3 the hex value is:

```
unsigned int mask = 0x08;
```

We now need to set GPIO Pin 3 to output, making sure not to change any of the other pins:

```
*dirset = mask;
```

We can now write a loop to toggle GPIO Pin 3 as fast as possible:

```
for (;;) {
      *outset = mask;
      *outclr = mask;
  }
```

The complete program is:

```
int main() {
 volatile unsigned int *dirset=(unsigned int *)(0x50000000UL+0x518);
 volatile unsigned int *outset=(unsigned int *)(0x50000000UL+0x508);
 volatile unsigned int *outclr=(unsigned int *)(0x50000000UL+0x50C);
 unsigned int mask = 1 << 3;
 *dirset = mask;
 for (;;) {
    *outset = mask;
    *outclr = mask;
 }
 return 0;
}
```

Notice that you don't have to include the micro:bit library to make this work.

If you run the program and measure the pulse widths you will find it is much faster:

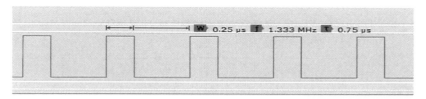

The pulse width is 0.25 microseconds compared to the 3.5 microsecond pulses we can generate using the framework, i.e. more than ten times faster.

This only leaves the question as to why the low time, 0.5 microseconds, is much longer than the high time?

The answer might surprise you. The extra time is how long it takes the end of the for loop to perform its loop end test and return to the start of the loop. The memory mapping instructions are now performing at the speed of the processor and the pulse train produced is influenced by the way the processor executes other instructions. You can't get rid of the time needed to transfer control to another part of the program to form a loop - a goto generates the same delay.

If you look more closely at the analyzer trace you will find that every now and again there is a pulse only 0.125 microseconds wide - presumably an artifact of the cache in use.

Rather than trying to work out exactly what is going on, the moral of the story is that when you are working at speeds that are close to the execution time of a single instruction you cannot expect it to be reproducible in a complex modern processor.

If you add busy wait loops to slow things down then the variations due to the processor become less important and the high time is equal to the low time:

```
volatile int i;
for (;;) {
    *outset = mask;
    for (i = 0; i < n; i++) {};
    *outclr = mask;
    for (i = 0; i < n; i++) {};
}
```

You can estimate the value of n using:

```
n=0.74*t+ 0.88
```

where t is in microseconds and is greater than or equal to 0.88 microseconds.

## Phased Pulses

There is another, almost more important, reason than speed for using direct access to the hardware. You can use direct access to set multiple GPIO lines at the same time so eliminating much of the synchronization problem encountered in the previous chapter.

For example to switch P0 and P1 in phase you would use:

```
unsigned int mask = 1 << 3 | 1 << 2;
*dirset = mask;
 volatile int i;
 for (;;) {
    *outset = mask;
     for (i = 0; i < 0; i++) {};
    *outclr = mask;
    for (i = 0; i < 0; i++) {};
}
```

Notice that Pin 1 on the edge connector is GPIO Pin 2 hence the mask setting bits 3 and 2.

If you try this out you will find that the two GPIO lines change at the same time:

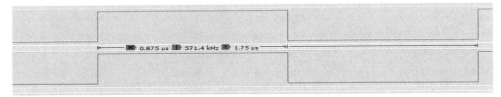

The next part, setting the lines in anti-phase, isn't so simple. The obvious approach is:

```
unsigned int mask = 1 << 3 | 1 << 2;
unsigned int mask1 = 1 << 3;
unsigned int mask2 = 1 << 2;
*dirset = mask;
volatile int i;
for (;;) {
    *outset = mask1;
    *outclr = mask2;
    for (i = 0; i < 0; i++) {};
    *outclr = mask1;
    *outset = mask2;
    for (i = 0; i < 0; i++) {};
}
```

In this case we set Pin 0 and Pin 1 in separate operations so they are switched at slightly different times.

If you look at a logic analyzer you will discover that there is a 0.25 microsecond overlap:

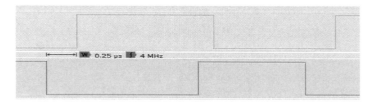

Better but not perfect. Perfection is slightly more complicated. To switch the two lines at the same time we need to work with the OUT register.

First we have to read it to establish the states of the other GPIO lines and then we have invert just bits 2 and 3 each time though the loop:

```
volatile unsigned int*out=(unsigned int *)(0x50000000UL + 0x504);
    unsigned int mask = 1 << 3 | 1 << 2;
    unsigned int mask1 = 1 << 3;
    unsigned int mask2 = 1 << 2;
    unsigned int tempmask = 0;
    *dirset = mask;

    *outset = mask1;
    *outclr = mask2;

    volatile int i;
    for (;;) {
        tempmask = *out ^ mask;
        *out = tempmask;
        for (i = 0; i < 0; i++) {};
    }
```

Notice that we need access to the OUT register so we need a new pointer. We still need mask1 and mask2 to set the two lines, one to high and one to low, before we start the loop.

In the loop all we do is read the OUT register and exclusive or it with mask - this flips bits 2 and 3 each time. Then we simply have to store the tempmask back in the out register and repeat. You can make this program shorter and slightly faster by not using temp mask but the gains aren't huge. Now the two lines switch in anti-phase together and the pulses are 1 microsecond:

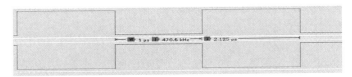

This is typical of the sort of thing you have to do if it is important that GPIO lines change state at the same time.

## How Fast Can Input Be?

The final question is how fast can we read the state of a line using memory mapped access? The answer can be found by repeating the program given in the previous chapter but using direct memory access rather than the framework.

In both cases we use the serial port to get the results and this means that we have to include the framework and instantiate at least a serial object. This causes a slight problem in that we now have to initialize the GPIO line we want to use more fully than just setting it to output as in the previous section.

Let's discover how fast a pulse interval can be measured:

```
#include "MicroBit.h"
MicroBitSerial serial(USBTX, USBRX);
int main() {
    volatile unsigned int*in=(unsigned int *)(0x50000000UL+0x510);
    volatile unsigned int*pin3=(unsigned int *)(0x50000000UL+0x70C);
    unsigned int mask = 1 << 3;
    *pin3=0x0;
    volatile int i;
    while (1) {
        while (mask == ((*in) & mask)) {};
        while (mask != ((*in) & mask)) {};
        for (i = 0; i < 5000; i++) {
            if (mask != ((*in) & mask)) break;
        }
        serial.printf("%d\n\r", i);
    }
    return 0;
}
```

This program is the same as the one in the previous chapter, but now P0 is being read using **(\*in)&mask** which is equal to mask if the pin is at a one level and equal to zero otherwise.

The line

```
*pin3=0x0;
```

sets the configuration of the pin to input and sets everything else to its default.

If you run the program you will find that the relationship between the loop counter n and pulse width is given by

```
t=1.12 n +0.32 microseconds
```

If you compare this to the result using the framework you will again find that you can read data about ten times faster. The formula works down to around 2 microseconds or slightly less. However, unless you need the additional speed it is better to use the framework. The techniques introduced in this chapter can be used to access other devices in the processor as well as the GPIO, but again in most cases it is safer to stay with the framework.

You might be tempted to write functions for the direct access of GPIO pins - don't, you will simply reinvent the framework.

If you are using direct memory access then you need the speed and using a function slows things down. The best option is to write C macros which place the same code inline in your program making things look neater but no slower. In practice writing good macros is difficult.

There is another way to make GPIO lines work even faster. The micro:bit's processor has internal hardware - GPIOTE and PPI - that make it possible to control the GPIO lines from events that occur in other peripherals without the processor being involved. Using this you can toggle a GPIO line at up to 8MHz, but the problem is controlling what it does other than generate a uniform pulse train. Using the GPIOTE and PPI for custom tasks is beyond the scope of this book, but we do meet them in the next chapter where they are used to implement Pulse Width Modulation, PWM.

# Chapter 5

# Pulse Width Modulation, Servos and more

One way around the problem of getting a fast response from a microcontroller is to move the problem away from the processor. In the case of the micro:bit's processor there are some built-in devices that can use GPIO lines to implement protocols without the CPU being involved. In this chapter we take a close look at pulse width modulation (PWM) including sound generation, driving LEDs and servos.

The GPIO lines at their most basic output function can be set high or low by the processor. How fast they can be set high or low depends on the speed of the processor.

Using the GPIO line in its Pulse Width Modulation (PWM) mode you can generate pulse trains up to 9.6MHz, i.e. pulses as short as just a little more than 0.1 microseconds.

The reason for the increase in speed is that the GPIO controls a pulse generator and, once set to generate pulses of a specific type, the pulse generator just gets on with it without needing any intervention from the GPIO line or the processor. In fact the pulse output can continue after your program has ended if you forget to reset it.

Of course, even though the PWM line can generate pulses as short as 0.1 microseconds, it can only change the pulses it produces each time that processor can modify it. For example, you can't use PWM to produce a single 0.1 microsecond pulse because you can't disable the PWM generator in just 0.1 microsecond.

## Some Basic micro:bit PWM Facts

There are some facts worth getting clear right from the start, although some of the meanings will only become clear as we progress.

First what is PWM?

The simple answer is that a Pulse Width Modulated signal has pulses that repeat at a fixed rate - say one pulse every millisecond but the width of the pulse can be changed.

There are two basic things to specify about the pulse train that is generated, its repetition rate and the width of each pulse. Usually the repetition rate is set as a simple repeat period and the width of each pulse is specified as a percentage of the repeat period the duty cycle. For example a 1ms repeat and a 50% duty cycle specifies a 1ms period which is high for 50% of the time, i.e. a pulse width of 0.5ms. The two extremes are 100% duty cycle, i.e. the line is always high; and 0% duty cycle, i.e. the line is always low.

What this means is that generally you select a repeat rate and stick to it and what you change as the program runs is the duty cycle.

In many cases PWM is implemented using special PWM generator hardware that is built either into the processor chip or provided by an external chip. The processor simply sets the repeat rate by writing to a register and then changes the duty cycle by writing to another register. This generally provides the best sort of PWM with no load on the processor and generally glitch-free operation. You can even buy add-on boards that will provide additional channels of PWM without adding to the load on the processor.

The alternative to dedicated PWM hardware is to implement it in software. You can quite easily work out how to do this. All you need a timing loop to set the line high at the repetition rate and then set it low again according to the duty cycle. You can implement this using either interrupts or a polling loop.

In the case of the micro:bit the PWM lines are not implemented using special PWM hardware. Instead two general purpose facilities - the GPIOTE and the PPI – are used to allow the GPIO lines to trigger events and respond to tasks. The software sets things up so that the system timer automatically toggles the specified GPIO line a the selected repetition rate and duty cycle. This saves the processor's time, but it is sophisticated and at times a little difficult to use.

You can use the three "main" GPIO lines, P0, P1 and P2, for PWM. You can also use P3, P4 and P10, but as these are also connected to the LED display they also make the LEDs flash - more of which in Chapter 14. For the moment we will concentrate on using P0, P1 and P2.

As a single timer is used, the repetition rate is shared between all of the GPIO lines being used as PWM outputs. That is, all PWM lines operate at the same frequency - i.e. the last frequency set.

You can, however, set different duty cycles for each of the PWM lines you are using by setting the repetition rate in multiples of 4 microseconds, i.e. the timer tick is 4 microseconds.

The fastest pulse repetition rate you can specify is 1 microsecond, but this actually gives a 27-microsecond repeat rate.

The slowest is 0.262 seconds which means you can't use a PWM line to flash an LED once every second.

As you can guess, there are no PWM inputs, just six outputs. If for some reason you need to decode or respond to a PWM input then you need to program it using the GPIO input lines and the pulse measuring techniques introduced in the previous chapters. If you are really ambitious you could use the GPIOTE and PPI facilities to automatically analyze the incoming PWM signal. Again you would use the timer to record the repetition rate and duty cycle.

## PWM Functions

The micro:bit framework attempts to provide PWM in easy to use forms. It provides functions which target the two main uses of PWM - DtoA conversion and controlling servo motors. More about both topics later in the chapter.

Instead of letting you specify a repeat rate and duty cycle the framework provides two sets of functions, one for working with an analog output and one for working with a servo. Of the two the analog output functions are the simpler and more direct. The more complex servo functions are described later in connection with implementing a servo driver.

You can set the repeat period using either:

```
int setAnalogPeriod(int period)
int setAnalogPeriodUs(int period)
```

The first sets the period in milliseconds and the second works in microseconds.

The next function sets the duty cycle, but not in an obvious way:

```
int setAnalogValue(int value)
```

The value can be anything between 0, corresponding to a duty cycle of 0%, and 1023, corresponding to 100%.

There is one small detail that you have to be aware of. The setAnalogValue function also sets up the pin for analog output if it isn't already set up. What this means is that you have to set an analog value before you set an analog period.

There are also two utility functions that let you read the current set period:

```
int getAnalogPeriod(int period)
int getAnalogPeriodUs(int period)
```

You can use these functions on P0, P1, P2, P3, P4 and P10 but, as already noted P3, P4 and P10 are connected to the LED display and are best avoided if possible for general PWM work.

Although you can set the repeat rate down to 1 microsecond, the PWM mechanism has a smallest time of around 27 microseconds and the timer tick is 4 microseconds, making this the maximum achievable precision.

| Set | Actual microseconds |
|-----|---------------------|
| 1 | 27 |
| 10 | 27 |
| 30 | 35 |
| 100 | 107 |
| 500 | 507 |
| 1000 | 1007 |

The longest time you can set is around 262 milliseconds, corresponding to the longest time a 32-bit timer running at 4 microseconds per tick can count to.

You could get different maximum and minimum rates by programming the timer yourself, but this is a difficult problem.

## Using PWM

So now you know how to make use of the PWM lines. All you have to do is set the value and the period.

The simplest PWM program you can write is:

```
#include "MicroBit.h"
MicroBit uBit;
int main() {
    uBit.init();
    uBit.io.P0.setAnalogValue(511);
    uBit.io.P0.setAnalogPeriod(1);
    release_fiber();
    return 0;
}
```

This produces a pulse train consisting of a millisecond wide pulse with a 50% duty cycle, i.e. high for 500 microseconds.

You have to set the value first and then set the period, otherwise the PWM line isn't setup properly. You also have to set the period for each pin you are using even if it does set the same period. Notice that there is no need to put the program into an infinite loop. Once the PWM line has been set up and enabled it just gets on with generating the pulse train, no matter what the micro:bit does. In this case the pulse generation continues long after the program has ended:

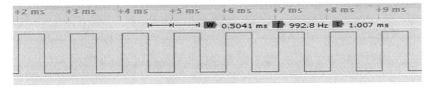

Just to demonstrate that multiple PWM lines can be used independently of one another, here is a program that sets each one of the three main PWM GPIO lines, P0, P1 and P2, to a different duty cycle:

```
#include "MicroBit.h"
MicroBit uBit;

int main() {
    uBit.init();
    uBit.io.P0.setAnalogValue(200);
    uBit.io.P1.setAnalogValue(511);
    uBit.io.P2.setAnalogValue(800);

    uBit.io.P0.setAnalogPeriod(1);
    uBit.io.P1.setAnalogPeriod(1);
    uBit.io.P2.setAnalogPeriod(1);

    release_fiber();
    return 0;
}
```

Notice that you have to set the value and then period for each pin you are using. You can see the result in the following logic analyzer display:

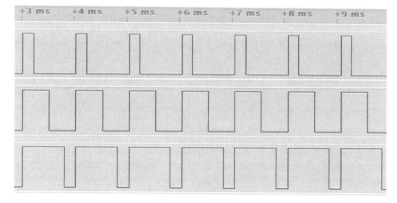

## How Fast Can You Modulate?

In most cases the whole point is to vary the duty cycle or the period of the pulse train for reasons that will be discussed later. This means that the next question is how fast can you change the characteristic of a PWM line? In other words, how fast can you change the duty cycle?

There is no easy way to give an exact answer and in most applications an exact answer isn't of much value. The reason is that for a PWM signal to convey information it generally has to deliver a number of complete cycles with a given duty cycle because of the way pulses are often averaged in applications.

We also have another problem - synchronization.

There is no way to swap from one duty cycle to another exactly when a complete duty cycle has just finished. What this means is that there is going to be a glitch when you switch from one duty cycle to another. Of course this glitch becomes less important as you slow the rate of duty cycle change and exactly what is useable depends on the application.

For example if you try changing the duty cycle about every 100 microseconds and the pulse width is 50 microseconds then you are going to see roughly two to three pulses per duty cycle:

```
volatile int i;
uBit.init();

uBit.io.P0.setAnalogValue(200);
uBit.io.P0.setAnalogPeriodUs(50);

for(;;){
  for(i=1;i<100;i++){};
  uBit.io.P0.setAnalogValue(200);
  for(i=1;i<100;i++){};
  uBit.io.P0.setAnalogValue(800);
}
```

This results in a fairly irregular pulse pattern:

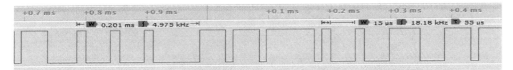

The timing of the change and the time it takes to make the change cause the glitches between duty cycles.

If you change the busy waits to n=1000 and generate duty cycle changes every millisecond or so then the pattern looks a lot better because you are going to see 19 to 20 pulses before each change, but the glitches are still there:

Is there anything that can be done about the glitching? Yes and no.

You can't do anything about 40 microseconds or so it takes to change from one duty cycle to another but you can synchronize when it happens to the timer using the **wait_us** function. If you swap the busy waits for the 100 microsecond delays to:

```
wait_us(100);
```

you will find that you do consistently get three pulses of each duty cycle, but separated by a longer pulse.

What all this is really about is trying to lower your expectation of how sophisticated you can be in using PWM on the micro:bit. The fastest PWM repetition rate that you can use is about 30 microseconds and to minimize the glitches you need to leave the duty cycle stable for 10 to 20 pulses i.e. about 200-600 microseconds. In many applications this is very acceptable but don't expect to use PWM to send coded data and using it for waveform synthesis as a DtoA converter is limited to around 4KHz.

## Uses of PWM - DtoA

What sorts of things do you use PWM for? There are lots of very clever uses for PWM, however there are two use cases which account for most PWM applications - voltage or power modulation and signaling to servos.

The amount of power delivered to a device by a pulse train is proportional to the duty cycle. A pulse train that has a 50% duty cycle is delivering current to the load only 50% of the time and this is irrespective of the pulse repetition rate.

So duty cycle controls the power but the period still matters in many situations because you want to avoid any flashing or other effects - a higher frequency smooths out the power flow at any duty cycle.

If you add a low pass filter to the output of a PWM signal then what you get is a voltage that is proportional to the duty cycle. This can be looked at in many different ways, but again it is the result of the amount of power delivered by a PWM signal. You can also think of it as using the filter to remove the high frequency components of the signal, leaving only the slower components due to the modulation of the duty cycle.

The framework's PWM functions are designed to allow you to use this as a crude DtoA converter and this is why the function is setValue and not setDuty cycle. It mimics the workings of an eight-bit AtoD converter. You set the duty cycle using a value in the range 0 to 1023 and you get a voltage output that is:

```
3.3*value/1023V
```

The only problem is that if your aim is to get a clean wave form you have a lot of work to do. The fastest pulse rate is around 50 microseconds and the usual rule of thumb is that you need ten pulses to occur per conversion, i.e. the maximum frequency you can produce is:

```
pulse rate/10
```

This means that the fastest signal you can create using the micro:bit is 1/500MHz or 2KHz, which isn't fast enough for a great many applications. In particular you can't use it for sound synthesis.

You also have 1024 voltage levels you can set. At 3.3V each step corresponds to about 300 micro Volts. This is unrealistic for many applications and setting the voltage to the nearest 300 milli Volts or greater is more sensible.

To demonstrate the sort of approach that you can use to DtoA conversion, the following program creates a triangle or ramp waveform:

```
#include "MicroBit.h"
MicroBit uBit;

int main() {
    int i;
    uBit.init();
    uBit.io.P0.setAnalogValue(200);
    uBit.io.P0.setAnalogPeriodUs(50);
    for(;;){
        for(i=0;i<1024;i=i+10){
                uBit.io.P0.setAnalogValue(i);
                wait_us(100);
        }
    }
    release_fiber();
    return 0;
}
```

The inner for loop sets values of 0 to 1024 in steps of 10, i.e. 300mV per step and the delay of 100 microseconds produces a total loop time of over 180 microseconds. This means that around three pulses of each duty cycle should be produced - which is far too few but it is interesting to see what happens. The waveform repeats after around 18 milliseconds, which makes the frequency around 66Hz. Using an oscilloscope, the measured repeat time is more like 20ms or 50Hz.

To see the analog wave form we need to put the digital output into a low pass filter. A simple resistor and capacitor work reasonably well - the cutoff frequency for the filter shown is 200Hz.

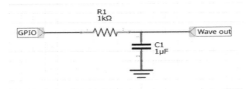

The filter's cut off is a little on the low side as can be seen by the slow fall to ground a the end of each waveform. However if you increase the cut off then even more irregularities show in the ramp. The reason for these irregularities is the short time each duty cycle is presented and the glitches that occur when changing duty cycle.

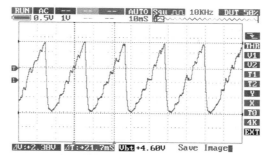

If you change the wait to 200 so that six or so duty cycles are presented then the result looks smoother and with fewer glitches:

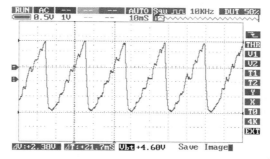

If you reduce the number of steps to 100 you get the same frequency back and a reasonably acceptable waveform:

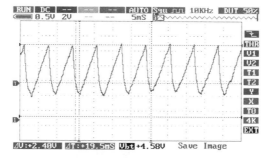

You can create a sine wave or any other waveform you need using the same techniques but 100Hz is a practical upper limit on what you can manage.

## Music

So how can the micro:bit generate musical notes?

The simplest solution is not to try to generate anything other than a square wave. That is, use the pulse period rather than duty cycle.

As the frequency of middle C is 261.6Hz, the period needed is roughly 3823 microseconds and so to generate middle C you could use

```
uBit.io.P0.setAnalogValue(511);
uBit.io.P0.setAnalogPeriodUs(3823);
```

The resulting output is a square wave, which isn't particularly nice to listen to. You can improve it by feeding it through a simple low pass filter like the one used for waveform synthesis. The correct values of R and C are a matter of taste, but 1uF to 0.1 and 1K work reasonably well.

The period t you need for any frequency f is:

```
t=1/f
```

and you can look up the frequencies for other notes and use a table to generate them.

## Controlling An LED

You can use a PWM supply to control the brightness of an LED for example, or the rotation rate of a DC motor. The only differences in applications such as these are to do with the voltage and current you need to control and the way duty cycle relates to what ever the physical effect is. In other words if you want to change some device by 50% how much do you need to change the duty cycle?

For example how do we "dim an LED"? By changing the duty cycle of the PWM pulse train you can set the amount of power delivered to an LED, or any other device, and hence change its brightness.

For example, for an LED we might use a 3.3V supply and a current of a few tens of milliamps. In the case of an LED the connection between duty cycle and brightness is a complicated matter, but the simplest approach uses the fact that the perceived brightness is roughly proportional to the cube of the input power. The exact relationship is more complicated, but this is good enough for most applications.

As the power supplied to the LED is proportional to the duty cycle we have:

```
b=kd³
```

where b is the perceived brightness and d is the duty cycle.

Notice that as the LED when powered by a PWM signal is either full on or full off, there is no effect of the change in LED light output with current - the LED is always run at the same current.

What all of this means is that if you want an LED to fade in a linear fashion you need to change the duty cycle in a non-linear fashion. Intuitively it means that changes when the duty cycle is small produce bigger changes in brightness than when the duty cycle is large.

For a simple example we need to connect a standard LED to the PWM line.

Given that all of the micro:bit's GPIO lines work at 3.3V and ideally only supply 0.5mA we need a transistor to drive the LED which typically draws 20mA.

You could use an FET of some sort, but for this sort of application an old-fashioned Bipolar Junction Transistor works very well and is cheap and available in a through-hole mount, i.e. it comes with wires.

Almost any general purpose npn transistor will work but the 2N2222 is very common:

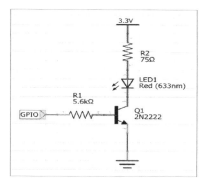

R1 restricts the current to 0.48mA, which is below the target 0.5mA, and assuming that the transistor has a minimum hfe of 50 this provides 24mA to power it. R2 limits the current to 20mA. Notice that these values are for a red LED with forward voltage drop of 1.8V and typical current 20mA. LEDs of different color have different forward voltage drops and currents.

If you are using the 2N2222 then the pin outs are:

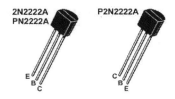

As always the positive terminal on the LED is the long pin.

Assuming that you have this circuit constructed then a simple PWM program to modify its brightness from low to high and back to low in a loop is;

```
#include "MicroBit.h"
MicroBit uBit;

int main() {
    uBit.init();
    uBit.io.P0.setAnalogValue(511);
    uBit.io.P0.setAnalogPeriodUs(1000);
    int w=1;
    int inc=1;
    for (;;) {
        uBit.io.P0.setAnalogValue(w);
        w=w+inc;
        if(w>1024 || w<=0)inc=-inc;
        wait_us(5000);
    }
    release_fiber();
    return 0;

)
```

The basic idea is to set up a pulse train with a period of 1ms. In the for loop the duty cycle is set to 0% to 100% and then back down to 0%. Notice that the way that the loop counts up and down is to use **inc** which is either 1 or -1 and using the age old trick of flipping between 1 and -1 and back again by multiplying by -1.

If you watch the flashing you will see that it changes brightness very quickly, and then seems to spend a long time "stuck" at almost full brightness, and then suddenly starts to dim rapidly. This is a consequence of the way the human eye perceives light output as a function of input power.

## Changing the LED brightness

What about a linear change in brightness?

To achieve this reasonably accurately isn't difficult all we need to do is increase the power or equivalently the duty cycle in steps that are cubic. If we just use 0 to 10 cubed we get a pulse width of 0 to 1000 which is ideal for our 1ms pulse used in the previous example i.e. 0 to close to 100% duty cycle.

If you need the ultimate speed you could precompute the powers but for simplicity we will just use integer multiplication:

```
#include "MicroBit.h"
MicroBit uBit;

int main() {
    uBit.init();
    uBit.io.P0.setAnalogValue(511);
    uBit.io.P0.setAnalogPeriodUs(1000);

    int w=0;
    int inc=1;
    for (;;) {
        uBit.io.P0.setAnalogValue(w*w*w);
        w=w+inc;
        if(w>10 || w<=0)inc=-inc;
        wait_us(50000);
    }
    release_fiber();
    return 0;
}
```

As this produces 10 cubic steps, a wait_us of 50000 makes each step last 5ms and so it takes 50ms to go from low to high.

If you try the program you should find that you see the LED increase steadily towards a maximum and then decrease steadily to a minimum.

If you replace the delay with a value of 100,000 you will get a 1-second cycle which, using only ten steps, starts to look a little flashy - not in a good sense.

You can increase the number of steps by simply dividing by a suitable factor. If you cube 1 to 20 you get 1 to 8000 and dividing by 8 gives 0 to 1000. Dividing by 8 is just a matter of three right shifts and so while not very accurate does allow fast computation with integer arithmetic:

```
    int w=0;
    int inc=1;
    for (;;) {
        uBit.io.P0.setAnalogValue((w*w*w)>>3);
        w=w+inc;
        if(w>20 || w<=0)inc=-inc;
        wait_us(50000);
    }
```

Notice that as there are now twice as many steps we only need each one to last half the time, i.e. 50,000 microseconds.

In most cases exactly how linear the response of the LED is is irrelevant - a rough approximation looks as smooth to the human eye. The only exception is when you are trying to drive LEDs to create a grey level or color display when color calibration is another level of accuracy.

## Controlling a Servo

Hobby servos, the sort used in radio control models, are very cheap and easy to use and the micro:bit has enough PWM lines to control three of them without much in the way of extras and without losing any other facilities. You can of course control more if you are prepared to sacrifice using the LED display.

A basic servo has just three connections - usually ground and power line and a signal line. The colors used vary but the power is usually red and the ground line is usually black or brown. The signal line is white, yellow or orange.

The power wire has to be connected to 5V supply capable of providing enough current to run the motor - anything up to 500mA or more depending on the servo. As the micro:bit only has a 3V supply you will need an additional power source. The good news is that the servo signal line generally needs very little current, although it does need to be switched between 0 and 5V using a PWM signal.

You can assume that the signal line needs to be driven as a voltage load and so the appropriate way to drive the servo is:

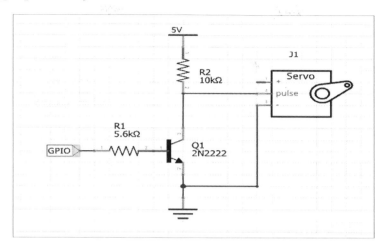

The resistor R1 can be a lot larger than 10K for most servos - 47K often works. The 5.6K resistor limits the base current to slightly less than 0.5mA. Pin 1 can be connected to the micro:bit's 5V supply or to a separate supply if you need more current.

Now all we have to do is set the PWM line to produce 20ms pulses with pulse widths ranging from 0.5 to 2.5 ms. You can do this using the PWM functions we have been using but the framework has a set of functions that are specifically for servo PWM control:

- `int setServoValue( int  value)`
- `int setServoValue( int  value,int range)`
- `int setServoValue( int  value,int range,int center)`

These set the duty cycle using a default pulse rate of 20ms. If for any reason you need a different pulse rate you can set it using:

```
int setServoPulseUs(int  pulseWidth)
```

The three forms of ServoValue function cater for different degrees of customization that the servo needs.

The first, setServoValue simply produces pulses with widths ranging from 500 microseconds to 2.5 milliseconds, which is what most servos work with, specified as a value from 0 to 180 corresponding to the normal 180 degree rotation of a servo.

The other two functions allow you to set the range and center value. If you specify a range and center then the angle selects a value in the range:

```
center-range/2 and center+range/2
```

If you only specify a range ten the default center of 1.5ms is used.

So the simplest servo program you can write is something like:

```
#include "MicroBit.h"
MicroBit uBit;


int main() {
    uBit.init();
    for (;;) {
        uBit.io.P0.setServoValue(0);
        uBit.sleep(1000);
        uBit.io.P0.setServoValue(90);
        uBit.sleep(1000);
        uBit.io.P0.setServoValue(180);
        uBit.sleep(1000);
    }
    release_fiber();
    return 0;
}
```

This moves the servo to three positions and pauses. If you run the program using the circuit given earlier, you will discover that the servo does nothing at all – apart, perhaps, from vibrating.

The reason is that the transistor voltage driver is an inverter. When the PWM line is high the transistor is fully on and the servo's pulse line is effectively grounded. When the PWM line is low the transistor is fully off and the servo's pulse line is pulled high by the resistor.

A common solution to this problem is to drive the servo using an emitter-follower configuration, but in this case this isn't possible because the maximum voltage generated by an emitter-follower configuration is:

$$3.3 - 0.6 = 2.7V$$

which is too low to drive most servos.

The standard solution in this case is to use two transistors to generate a non-inverted pulse, but it is possible to use a single transistor in a non-inverting configuration.

The simplest solution of all is to ignore the problem in hardware and solve the problem in software. Instead of generating 20ms pulses with pulse widths 0.5 to 2.5ms, you can generate an inverted pulse with 20ms pulses with widths in the range 17.5 to 19 ms. To do this we have to go back to using the non-servo PWM functions. The principle is that if the servo needs a 10% duty cycle we supply it with a 90% duty cycle which the inverter converts back to a 10% duty cycle.

The range of duty cycles we need goes from 17.5 to 19.5.ms which in percentages is 87.5% to 97.5% or as values 895 to 997.

Simple math can convert an angle T to a value in the range 895 to 997:

$$value = (997\text{-}895)/180 * T + 895$$
$$= 138 * T/180 + 895$$

To make sure this works with all servos it is a good idea to restrict the range to 1ms to 2ms, or inverted 18ms to 19ms, and hence values from 920 to 972:

$$value = 52 * T/190 + 920$$

So we can write the same testing program as:

```
#include "MicroBit.h"
MicroBit uBit;

int main() {
    uBit.init();
    uBit.io.P0.setAnalogValue(0);
    uBit.io.P0.setAnalogPeriod(20);
  for (;;) {
    uBit.io.P0.setAnalogValue(52 * 0 / 180 + 920);
    uBit.sleep(1000);
    uBit.io.P0.setAnalogValue(52 * 90 / 180 + 920);
    uBit.sleep(1000);
    uBit.io.P0.setAnalogValue(52 * 180 / 180 + 920);
    uBit.sleep(1000);
  }
  release_fiber();
  return 0;
}
```

If you run this program you should find that the servo moves as promised. However, it might not reach its limits of movement. Servos differ in how they respond to the input signal and you might need to calibrate the pulse widths. Many robot implementations, for example, calibrate the servos to find their maximum movement using either mechanical switches to detect when the servo is at the end of its range or a vision sensor.

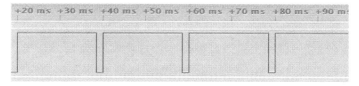

You can see from the logic analyzer plot that the PWM pulse train at the GPIO pin is "inverted" as desired:

You can also see that the values used for the period and for the pulse width could do with some adjustment to bring them closer to the target values. In practice, however, servo calibration is the better answer.

## Non-Inverting Drivers

The software solution to driving a servo via a simple inverting buffer is elegant, if slightly messy when it comes to computing the duty cycle needed. The traditional solution is to use two transistors to create a non-inverting buffer:

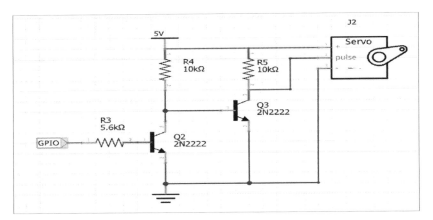

There is a way to use a single transistor as a non-inverting buffer using a common base configuration:

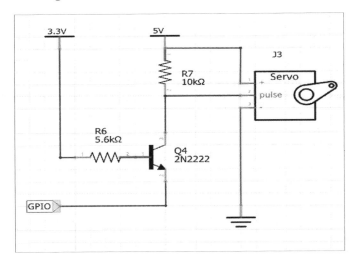

In this variation on a common base mode the transistor's base is connected to the 3.3V line and its collector to the 5V supply. Note that the two power supplies have to share a common earth.

If the GPIO output is low then R6 sets the base emitter voltage to 0.6V and the transistor is hard on, pulling the output to the servo low.

If the GPIO output is high the base emitter voltage is zero and the transistor is cut off, making the output to the servo high.

You can see that this is non-inverting, but the problem is that the current that flows through R7 is also the emitter current, which is the current the GPIO line has to sink. What this means is that the current in R7 is limited to around 1mA and this circuit provides no amplification. Of course, you could add another transistor to provide current amplification, but in this case you would be better off going back to the standard 2-transistor arrangement.

This circuit does, however, work with most servos so in this role it is useful. The current in the GPIO line is 1mA and should be driven in strong mode, but it does work in standard mode if you just want to test things out.

Here is a "non-inverted" version of the test program given earlier. The range of duty cycle is limited to 1ms to 2ms to make sure it works with all servos. Change the range or center value to make it work with your servo:

```
#include "MicroBit.h"
MicroBit uBit;

int main() {
    uBit.init();
    for (;;) {
        uBit.io.P0.setServoValue(0,1000);
        uBit.sleep(1000);
        uBit.io.P0.setServoValue(90,1000);
        uBit.sleep(1000);
        uBit.io.P0.setServoValue(180,1000);
        uBit.sleep(1000);
    }
    release_fiber();
    return 0;
}
```

## What Else Can You Use PWM For?

PWM lines are incredibly versatile and it is always worth asking the question "could I use PWM?" when you are considering almost any problem.

The LED example shows how you can use PWM as a power controller. You can extend this idea to a computer controlled switch mode power supply. All you need is a capacitor to smooth out the voltage and perhaps a transformer to change the voltage.

You can also use PWM to control the speed of a DC motor and if you add a simple bridge circuit you can control its direction and speed.

Finally, you can use a PWM signal as a modulated carrier for data communications. For example, most infrared controllers make use of a 38KHz carrier, which is roughly 26 microseconds. This is switched on and off for 1 millisecond and this is well within the range that the PWM can manage. So all you have to do is replace the red LED in the previous circuit with an infrared LED and you have the start of a remote control or data transmission link.

The I2C bus is one of the most useful ways of connecting moderately sophisticated sensors and peripherals to the any processor. The only problem is that it can seem like a nightmare confusion of hardware, low-level interaction and high-level software. There are few general introductions to the subject because at first sight every I2C device is different, but here we present one.

I2C is a serial bus that can be used to connect multiple devices to a controller. It is a simple bus that uses two active wires - one for data and one for a clock. Despite there being lots of problems in using the I2C bus, because it isn't well standardized and devices can conflict and generally do things in their own way, it is still commonly used and too useful to ignore.

The big problem in getting started with the I2C bus is that you will find it described at many different levels of detail - the physical bus characteristics, the protocol, the details of individual devices. It can be difficult to relate all of this together and produce a working anything.

In fact you only need to know the general workings of the I2C bus, some general features of the protocol and know the addresses and commands used by any particular device.

To explain and illustrate these idea we really do have to work with a particular device to make things concrete. However the basic stages of getting things to work, testing and verification are more or less the same irrespective of the device.

It is worth mentioning that the micro:bit has two devices already connected to its I2C bus - the accelerometer and the magnetometer and we need to look at how these work as a separate topic.

## I2C Hardware Basics

The I2C bus is very simple. It consists of just two signal lines SDA and SCL, the data and clock lines respectively. Each siignal line is pulled up by a suitable resistor to the supply line at whatever voltage the devices are working at - 3.3V and 5V are common choices, The size of the pullup resistors isn't critical, but 4.7K is typical.

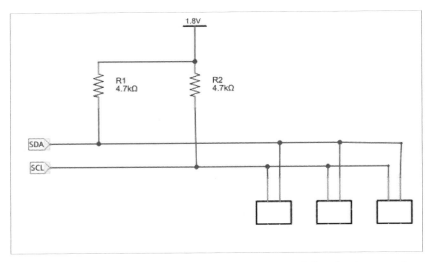

You simply connect the SDA and SCL pins of each of the devices to the pull up resistors. Of course if any of the devices have built-in pullup resistors you can omit the external resistors. More of a problem is if multiple devices each have pull ups. In this case you need to disable all but one set.

The I2C bus is an open collector bus. This means that it is actively pulled down by a transistor set to on. When the transistor is off, however, the bus returns to the high voltage state via the pullup resistor. The advantage of this approach is that multiple devices can pull the bus low at the same time. That is an open collector bus is low when one or more devices pulls it low and high when none of the devices is active.

The SCL line provides a clock which is used to set the speed of data transfer - one data bit is presented on the SDA line for each pulse on the SCL line. In all cases the master drives the clock line to control how fast bits are transferred. The slave can however hold the clock line low if it needs to slow down the data transfer.

In most cases the I2C bus has a single master device - the micro:bit in our case - which drives the clock and invites the slaves to receive or transmit data. Multiple masters are possible, but this is advanced and not often necessary.

At this point we could go into the details of how all of this works in terms of bits. However, the framework handles these details for us. All you really need to know is that all communication occurs in 8-bit packets.

The master sends a packet, an address frame, which contains the address of the slave it wants to interact with. Every slave has to have a unique address - usually 7 bits but it can be 11 bits, but the micro:bit does not support this.

One of the problems in using the I2C bus is that manufacturers often use the same address or same set of selectable addresses and this can make using particular combinations of devices on the same bus difficult or impossible.

The 7-bit address is set as the high order 7 bits in the byte and this can be confusing as an address that is stated as 0x40 in the data sheet results in 0x80 being sent to the device. The low order bit of the address signals a write or a read operation depending on whether it is a zero or a one respectively.

After sending an address frame, the master sends or receives data frames back from the slave, There are also special signals used to mark the start and end of an exchange of packets, but the framework takes care of these.

This is really all you need to know about I2C in general to get started, but it is worth finding out more of the details as you need them. You almost certainly will need them as you debug I2C programs.

## Micro:bit I2C

The micro:bit's processor has two built-in I2C masters. Each one can be connected to any of the GPIO pins - that is any two GPIO pins can be used as SCL and SDA. However the micro:bit's accelerometer and magnetometer make use of GPIO 0 and 20 which are brought out as edge connector pins P19 SCL and P20 SDA. These pins are configured in mode S0D1, i.e. they are open collector and pull-up resistors are provided on the board.

You can use one of the I2C devices to work with the accelerometer or magnetometer and the other can be used externally.

The hardware can work at 100kHz or 400kHz and supports clock stretching, see later. It isn't possible for another master to be on the bus with the micro:bit.

## The I2C Functions

You can either use the supplied **uBit.i2c** object or you can create your own using the constructor. As always if you create your own make sure it is a global object and don't create or initialize the uBit object:

```
MicroBitI2C( PinName  sda, PinName  scl)
```

For the standard I2C pins use:

```
MicroBitI2C i2c(I2C_SDA0, I2C_SCL0);
```

In most cases it is better to use the standard pins if you want to avoid problems with the accelerometer and magnetometer.

Each device on the I2C bus has to have a unique 7-bit address. You can look up the address that each device responds to in its datasheet.

Don't worry about any of the low-level descriptions of the way the least significant bit is used to determine if a read or a write is in operation - this is often reported in datasheets as one address for write and one for read. You also need to keep in mind that the 7-bit address is sent as the high order bits in the byte.

For example, a device might report an address of 0x40 on its data sheet. On the bus this would translate to a write address of 0x80 for write and a read address of 0x81 i.e. to write device 0x40 you use 0x80 and to write to it you use 0x81.

## Write

There are two write functions:

```
int write(int address,const char * data, int length)
int write(int address,const char *  data, int length,bool repeated)
```

What happens when you use one of these is that first an address frame is transmitted. The address frame is a byte containing the address of the device you specified. Notice that the 7-bit address has to be shifted into the top most bits and the first bit has to be zeroed. So to write to a device with an address of 0x40 you would use 0x80, or equivalently 0x40<<1.

After the address frame as many data frames are sent as you specified in data and length. Notice that a multibyte write involves sending a single address frame. This means there is a difference between trying to send a block of data one byte at a time, which repeats the address frame, and sending it in one go.

If you know about the I2C protocol, it is worth saying that the framework deals with the start sequence and the address frame, it checks the NACK/ACK bit from the slave, sends the data bits, checks the NACK/ACK bit from the slave and sends the stop sequence. That is, in normal use, the write transaction sending n bytes is:

```
START|  ADDR  |ACK|DATA0|ACK|DATA1|ACK|...|DATAn|ACK|STOP
```

Notice that it is the slave that sends the ACK bit and if the data is not received correctly it can send NACK instead.

A multibyte transfer is quite different from sending n single bytes one at a time.

```
START|  ADDR  |ACK|DATA0|ACK|STOP
START|  ADDR  |ACK|DATA1|ACK|STOP
...
START|  ADDR  |ACK|DATA1|ACK|STOP
```

You can opt not to send a STOP bit at the end of the write by setting the repeat parameter to true. That is, you can arrange to send multiple START bits, address frames and data as long as the entire sequence finishes with one STOP bit, which releases the bus. For multiple writes there is very little point in doing this apart from to keep control of the bus in multi-master setups. However, when you mix reads and writes things become a little more complicated, see the next section.

A very standard interaction between master and slave is writing data to a register. Many devices have internal storage, indeed some I2C devices are nothing but internal storage, e.g.. I2C EPROMs. In this case a standard transaction is:

1. send address frame
2. send a data frame with the command to select the register
3. send a data frame containing the byte or word to be written to the register

So, for example, you might use:

```
char buf[]={register,data};
write(address,buf,2);
```

Notice the command that has to be sent depends on the device and you have to look it up in its datasheet.

Next we have to look at how to read data from the device. Notice that in many transactions a read has to be preceded by a write that tells the device what data you want.

## Read

There are two read functions and they broadly copy the write functions:

```
int read ( int address,char * data, int length)
int read ( int address,char * data, int length,bool repeated)
```

They send an address frame and then read as many bytes from the slave as specified. In this case the address has to be shifted up one bit and the lower order bit set to one to indicate a read operation.

As with the write function, the framework takes care of all of the protocol necessary to send and receive the packets, including adding the one to the end of the address. The read transaction is:

START| ADDR |ACK|DATA0|ACK|DATA1|ACK|...|DATAn|NACK|STOP

The master sends the address and the slave sends the ACK after the address to acknowledge that it has been received and it is ready to send data. Then the slave sends bytes one at a time and the master sends ACK in response to each byte. Finally, the master sends a NACK to indicate that the last byte has been read and then a STOP bit. That is the master controls how many bytes are transferred. As in the case of the write functions, a block transfer of n bytes is different from transferring n bytes one at a time.

A very standard transaction is to read a register. As in the case of writing a register this involves sending the address and a command to select the register, but then you need to read the returned data. This requires the address frame to be sent again.

That is, to read a register you need a complete write and a complete read operation. So, for example, to read a register, with address reg, you would use something like:

```
char buf[]={reg};
write(address,buf,1);
read(address,buf,1);
```

If the register sends multiple bytes then you can sometimes read these one after another without sending an address frame each time as a block transfer.

In this case the transaction is:

START| ADDR |ACK|register|ACK|STOP|START|ADDR|ACK|data|NACK|STOP

Notice that there is a STOP followed by a START in the middle of the transaction. In principle a STOP frees the bus and another master could take over or the current master could start talking to a different device before issuing the next START to read the register.

In theory, and mostly in practice, a multiple interaction with a slave can work with a STOP-START separating each transaction or just repeated START bit and a STOP only at the very end of the transaction.

However, you will find that some slave devices state that they need a repeated START bit and no STOP bits in continued transactions. In this case you need to be careful how you send and receive data.

For example, to read a register from a device that requires repeated START bits but no STOP bit you would use:

```
char buf[]={reg};
write(address,buf,1,true);
read(address,buf,1);
```

This would send an address frame, the register address and then a START bit without a STOP, read the data from the slave and finally send a NAK and a STOP.

START| ADDR |ACK|register|ACK|START|ADDR|ACK|data|NACK|STOP

In practice it usually doesn't make any difference if you send a STOP bit in the middle of a write/read transaction, but you need to know about it just in case.

## Slow Read

This raises for the first time the question of how we cope with the speed that a slave can or cannot respond to a request for data.

There are two broad approaches to waiting for data on the I2C bus.

The first is simply to request the data and then perform reads in a polling loop. If the device isn't ready with the data then it sends a data frame with a

NACK bit set. The read functions return a MICROBIT_I2C_ERROR if it fails or MICROBIT_OK if it works.

Of course, the polling loop doesn't have to be "tight". The response time is often long enough to do other things and you can use the I2C bus to work with other slave devices while the one you activated gets on with trying to get the data you requested. All you have to do is to remember to read its data at some later time.

The second way is to allow the slave to hold the clock line low after the master has released it. In most cases the master will simply wait before moving on to the next frame while the clock line is held low. The micro:bit I2C bus implements this clock stretching protocol and it will wait until the slave releases the clock line before proceeding. This is very simple and it means you don't have to implement a polling loop, but also notice that your program is frozen until the slave releases the clock line.

Many devices implement both types of slow read protocol and you can use whichever suits your application.

There is also the small matter of the speed of the I2C clock. Most slave devices don't have a strict clock rate as they are designed as static devices synced to whatever SCL clock rate the master cares to use. If it turns out to be too fast then most will use clock stretching. In extreme cases it may be necessary to slow down the slave device, or even speed up the master's clock.

By default the I2C clock is run at 100K and there is no function that you can use to change it within the framework. However you can use the inherited

```
frequency(int hz);
```

but notice that hz can only be one of 100000, 250000 or 400000. If you use anything else the nearest standard value is used.

## Using The Built-in Devices

As already mentioned there are two built-in I2C devices, the accelerometer and the magnetometer. The framework provides special functions that work with both of these devices and these are the ones to use to work with either device. The way that these work is fairly straightforward and you can find out more from the documentation.

However we can use them as an example of how to work with I2C without having to use any special purpose hardware.

The accelerometer is a **MMA8653** and you can find out how it works from its data sheet. It has I2C address 0x1D.

The magnetometer is a **NXP MAG3110** and its data sheet reveals that it has I2C address 0x0E. Of the two devices, the magnetometer is the simpler and so it provides a better introductory example.

If you examine its data sheet you will find a table of registers:

| Name | Type | Address | Default | Comment |
|---|---|---|---|---|
| DR_STATUS | R | 0x00 | 0000 000 | Data ready status per axis |
| OUT_X_MSB | R | 0x01 | (0x03) | Bits [15:8] of X measurement |
| OUT_X_LSB | R | 0x02 | | Bits [7:0] of X measurement |
| OUT_Y_MSB | R | 0x03 | (0x05) | Bits [15:8] of Y measurement |
| OUT_Y_LSB | R | 0x04 | | Bits [7:0] of Y measurement |
| OUT_Z_MSB | R | 0x05 | (0x07) | Bits [15:8] of Z measurement |
| OUT_Z_LSB | R | 0x06 | | Bits [7:0] of Z measurement |
| WHO_AM_I | R | 0x07 | 0xC4 | Device ID Number |
| SYSMOD | R | 0x08 | data | Current System Mode |
| OFF_X_MSB | R/W | 0x09 | 0000 000 | Bits [14:7] of user X offset |
| OFF_X_LSB | R/W | 0x0A | 0000 000 | Bits [6:0] of user X offset |
| OFF_Y_MSB | R/W | 0x0B | 0000 000 | Bits [14:7] of user Y offset |
| OFF_Y_LSB | R/W | 0x0C | 0000 000 | Bits [6:0] of user Y offset |
| OFF_Z_MSB | R/W | 0x0D | 0000 000 | Bits [14:7] of user Z offset |
| OFF_Z_LSB | R/W | 0x0E | 0000 000 | Bits [6:0] of user Z offset |
| DIE_TEMP | R | 0x0F | data | Temperature, signed 8 bits in C |
| CTRL_REG1 | R/W | 0x10 | 0000 0000 | Operation modes |
| CTRL_REG2 | R/W | 0x11 | 0000 0000 | Operation modes |

The comments give you a general idea of what each register is for. For example, the WHO_AM_I register has address 0x07, is read only and has default value 0x0C. This is a good register for trying out the I2C commands because we know what the result should be.

The address of the device is 0x0E and so the address shifted left by one is 0x1C.. The register's address is 0x07. The data sheet also says that the device needs a repeated START bit for a register read, i.e. a STOP bit only at the end of the transaction:

```
#include "MicroBit.h"
MicroBit uBit;

int main() {
    uBit.init();
    char buf[]={0x07};
    uBit.i2c.write(0x1C,buf,1,true);
    uBit.i2c.read(0x1C,buf,1);
    printf("Id %X\r\n",(int)buf[0]);
    release_fiber();
    return 0;
}
```

If you connect a logic analyzer to Pin 19 and Pin 20 then you can see the transaction in action - you will also see some other transactions as the framework initializes the two built-in devices:

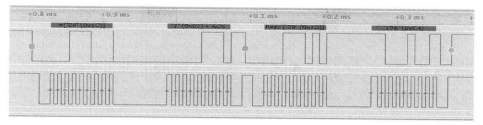

You can see that there is no STOP bit in the middle of the transaction, only at the end. While this is the way that the transaction should be done you will discover that if you take out the "true" in the write you will find little difference. The same data is provided by the slave and the only noticeable difference is slightly longer pauses between write and read transactions.

Now that we can read the ID of the device it is interesting to read some real data. First, however, we can make use of the framework's compass functions to get data from the device so that we know what results to expect.

The first part of the program gets the magnetic field in the x,y and z directions and prints them to the serial port:

```
uBit.init();
uBit.compass.updateSample();
int x = uBit.compass.getX();
printf("x %d \r\n", x);
int y = uBit.compass.getY();
printf("y %d \r\n", y);
int z = uBit.compass.getZ();
printf("z %d \r\n", z);
```

We can repeat the readings, but this time using I2C functions to talk directly to the device. If you consult the data sheet you will discover that the x,y,z data is stored in six single byte-registers with addresses starting at 0x01.

You can read these values one at a time but the device also supports a multibyte mode that will transfer all six bytes in one operation.

All you have to do is read six bytes from register 0x01 and you get the x, y and z data:

```
char buf = {0x01};
char buf2[7];
uBit.i2c.write(0x1C, buf, 1, true);
uBit.i2c.read(0x1C , buf2, 6);
int i;
for (i = 0; i < 6; i++) {
    printf("data %d %X\r\n", i, (int) buf2[i]);
}
```

The program prints the raw data to the serial port. We can convert the raw bytes to 16-bit signed values by packing them into suitable integers:

```
int16_t X = buf2[0] << 8 | buf2[1];
printf("X %d \r\n", X);
int16_t Y = buf2[2] << 8 | buf2[3];
printf("Y %d \r\n", Y);
int16_t Z = buf2[4] << 8 | buf2[5];
printf("Z %d \r\n", Z);
```

If you try this program you will discover that the framework gives slightly different results because it uses a different set of coordinates - all values are multiplied by 100 and the y and z values are multiplied by -1.

You can look up the data sheet of the accelerometer and access both devices using I2C, but the framework provides a comprehensive and easy to use set of functions for most tasks.

# Chapter 7

# I2C Measuring Temperature And Humidity

Using I2C devices is fairly easy once you have successfully used one and hence know what information you need and what to look for in a working system. In this chapter we use the HTU21D temperature and humidity sensor as a case study of I2C in action. It also happens to be a useful sensor.

Using an I2C device has two problems - the physical connection between master and slave and figuring out what the software has to do to make it work. In this chapter we take the principle outlined in the previous one and add information from the HTU21D data sheet to make a working temperature humidity sensor using the framework I2C functions.

First the hardware.

## The SparkFun HTU21D

The HTU21D Humidity and Temperature sensor provides an attractive way to make environmental measurements in a very small package and is one of the easiest of I2C devices to use.

Its only problem is that it is only available in a surface mount package. You could overcome this simply by soldering some wires onto the pads or with a general breakout board. However, it is much simpler to buy the SparkFun HTU21D breakout board – it's easy connections and built-in pull up resistors mean you don't need to add any components to get this circuit working. You just make four connections.

If you decide to work with some other I2C device you can still follow the steps in this account, but you would have to modify what you do to be correct for the device you are using. In particular if you select a device that works at 5V you might need a level converter.

### Wiring the HTU21D

In the first instance we can use the same I2C bus that the accelerometer and magnetometer are connected to.

| Physical Pin | Function |
|---|---|
| Pin 20 | SDA |
| Pin 19 | SCL |

Given that the HTU21D has pull up resistors we really should disable them when used on the internal I2C bus which already has pullups. In practice the additional pullups don't seem to make much difference to the waveforms and you can leave them in place while testing. Later when we try the same device on a separate bus the pulls will be required.

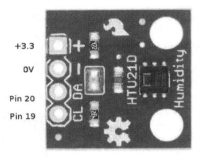

You can use a prototype board to make the connections and this makes it easier to connect other instruments such as a logic analyzer.

## A First Program

After wiring up any I2C device the first question that needs to be answered is, does it work? Unfortunately for most complex devices finding out if it works is a multi-step process. Our first program will aim to read some data back from the HTU21D - any data will do.

If you look at the data sheet you will find that the device address is 0x40 and it supports the following commands:

| Command | Code | Comment |
|---|---|---|
| Trigger Temperature Measurement | 0xE3 | Hold master |
| Trigger Humidity Measurement | 0xE5 | Hold master |
| Trigger Temperature Measurement | 0xF3 | No Hold master |
| Trigger Humidity Measurement | 0xF5 | No Hold master |
| Write user register | 0xE6 | |
| Read user register | 0xE7 | |
| Soft Reset | 0xFE | |

The easiest of these to get started with is the Read user register command. The user register gives the current setup of the device and can be used to set the resolution of the measurement.

Notice that the codes that you send to the device can often be considered addresses or commands. In this case you can think of sending 0xE7 as a command to read the register or the read address of the register - it makes no difference. In most cases the term command is used when sending the code makes the device do something and the term address is used when it simply makes the device read or write specific data.

To read the user register we have to write a byte containing 0xE7 and then read the byte the device sends back. This involves sending an address frame, a data frame and then another address frame and reading a data frame. The device seems to be happy if you send a STOP bit between each transaction or just a new START bit.

A program to read the user register is fairly easy to put together. The address of the device is 0x40 so its write address is 0x80 and its read address is 0x81. As the framework I2C functions add the lower bit, we simply use 0x80 as the device's address:

```
char buf[] = {0xE7};
uBit.i2c.write(0x80, buf, 1);
uBit.i2c.read(0x80, buf,1);
printf("User Register = %X \r\n",buf[0]);
```

This sends the address frame for 0x80 and then the data byte 0xE7 to select the user register. Next it sends an address frame for 0x81 to read the data.

If you run the program you will see:

```
Register= 02
```

this is the default value of the register and it corresponds to a resolution of 12 and 14 bits for the humidity and temperature respectively and a supply voltage greater than 2.25V.

## The I2C Protocol In Action

If you have a logic analyzer that can interpret the I2C protocol connected, what you will see is:

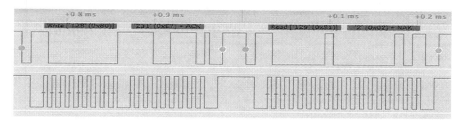

You can see that the write_byte function sends an address packet set to the device's 7-bit address 0x40 as the high order bits and the low order bit set to zero to indicate a write. After this you get a data packet sent containing the address of the register, 0xE7. After a few microseconds it sends the address frame again only this time with the low order bit set to 1 to indicate a read and it then receives back a single byte of data from the device, 0x02.

This all demonstrates that the external device is working properly and we can move on to getting some data of interest.

## Reading Raw Temperature Data

Now we come to reading one of the two quantities that the device measures, temperature. If you look back at the command table you will see that there are two possible commands for reading the temperature:

| Command | Code | Comment |
|---|---|---|
| Trigger Temperature Measurement | 0xE3 | Hold master |
| Trigger Temperature Measurement | 0xF3 | No Hold master |

What is the difference between Hold master and No Hold master?

This was discussed in the previous chapter in a general context. The device cannot read the temperature instantaneously and the master can either opt to be held waiting for the data, i.e. hold master, or released to do something else and poll for the data until it is ready.

The hold master option works by allowing the device to stretch the clock pulse by holding the line low after the master has released it. In this mode the master will wait until the device releases the line. Not all masters support this mode but the micro:bit does and this makes this the simplest option. To read the temperature using the Hold master mode you simply send 0xE3 and then read three bytes:

```
char buf[4] = {0xE3};
uBit.i2c.write(0x80, buf, 1);
uBit.i2c.read(0x80, buf,3);
uint8_t msb=buf[0];
uint8_t lsb=buf[1];
uint8_t check=buf[2];
printf("msb %d \n lsb %d \n checksum %d \n\r", msb,lsb,check);
```

The buffer is unpacked into three variables with more meaningful names: msb - most significant byte; lsb - least significant byte; check - checksum.

You should see something like:

```
msb 97
lsb 232
checksum 217
```

with the temperature in the 20C range.

The logic analyzer reveals what is happening.

First we send the usual address frame and write the 0xE3. Then after a short pause the read address frame is sent and the clock line is held low by the device (lower trace):

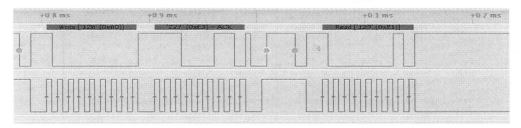

The clock line is held low by the device for over 42ms while it gets the data ready. It is released and the three data frames are sent:

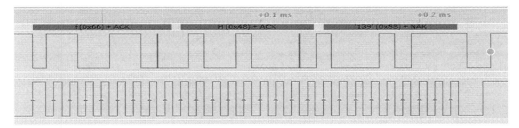

This response is a long way down the logic analyzer's trace so keep scrolling until you find it.

While clock stretching is the most simple, it sometimes doesn't work with some slave and master combinations.

Finally we have to find out how to use the No hold master mode or polling method of reading the data - it is sometimes useful although not in the case of the micro:bit.

In this case we can't use the single read_bytes_data command because the data will not be ready to read and the master will not be forced to wait for it. We have to use the two-step send the command and read the data approach:

```
char buf[4] = {0xF3};
uBit.i2c.write(0x80, buf, 1);
while (uBit.i2c.read(0x80, buf, 3) == MICROBIT_I2C_ERROR) {
};
```

In theory this polls repeatedly until the data is returned. In practice it doesn't work. The reason is that there is a fault in the hardware which causes it to lock up. The framework tries to compensate for this by resetting the I2C bus and retrying whenever it detects a NACK. The result is that the data is lost.

In short, you can't use polling on with the micro:bit.

## Processing the Data

Our next task isn't really directly related to the problem of using the I2C bus, but it is a very typical next step. The device returns the data in three bytes, but the way that this data relates to the temperature isn't simple.

If you read the data sheet you will discover that the temperature data is the 14-bit value that results by putting together the most and least significant byte and zeroing the bottom two bits. The bottom two bits are used as status bits - bit zero currently isn't used and bit one is a 0 if the data is a temperature measurement and a 1 if it is a humidity measurement.

To put the two bytes together we use:

```
unsigned int data16=((unsigned int) msb << 8) | (unsigned
int) (lsb & 0xFC);
```

This zeros the bottom two bits, shifts the msb up eight bits and ORs the two together. The result is a 16-bit temperature value with the bottom two bits zeroed.

Now we have raw temperature value, but we have still have to convert it to standard units. The datasheet gives the formula

```
Temp in C = -46.85 + 175.72 * data16 / 2¹⁶
```

The only problem in implementing this is working out $2^{16}$. You can work out $2^x$ with the expression 1<<x, i.e. shift 1 x places to the left.

This gives:

```
float temp = (float)(-46.8 +(175.72 *data16/(float)(1<<16)));
```

As $2^{16}$ is a constant that works out to 65536, it is more efficient to write:

```
float temp = (float)(-46.85 +(175.72 *data16/(float)65536));
```

Note the use of floating point arithmetic. The micro:bits's processor doesn't have hardware floating point but the framework comes with a software implementation. Floating point arithmetic is slow and it is usual to try to convert it into suitably scaled integer arithmetic.

In this case using floating point is convenient, but there is a snag. The printf function doesn't support floating point format. There is another "full" version which does, but this has to be imported into the build.

Overall it is easier to work in scaled integer - in this case temperature times 100 – so multiply the expression for temperature by 100 and make use of the fact that dividing by $2^{16}$ is the same as 16 right shifts:

```
int temp= -4685+((17572*data16)>>16);
```

Now all we have to do is print the temperature as a correctly scaled decimal value:

```
printf("Temperature %d.%d C \n\r",temp/100,temp%100);
```

The final program is:

```
#include "MicroBit.h"
MicroBit uBit; int main() {

    uBit.init();
    char buf[4] = {0xE3};
    uBit.i2c.write(0x80, buf, 1);
    uBit.i2c.read(0x80, buf, 3);
    uint8_t msb = buf[0];
    uint8_t lsb = buf[1];
    uint8_t check = buf[2];
    printf("\n\rmsb %d \n\rlsb %d \n\rchecksum %d \n\r",
                                    msb, lsb, check);
    unsigned int data16 = ((unsigned int) msb << 8) |
                            (unsigned int) (lsb & 0xFC);
    int temp = -4685 + ((17572 * data16) >> 16);
    printf("Temperature %d.%d C \n\r", temp / 100, temp % 100);
    release_fiber();
    return 0;
}
```

# Reading the Humidity

The nice thing about I2C and using a particular I2C device is that it gets easier. Once you have seen how to do it with one device the skill generalizes and once you know how to deal with a particular device other aspects of the device are usually similar.

To read the humidity we can more or less use the same program, we just need to change the command and the formula for the final percentage humidity. The command needed to read the three data bytes is 0xE5 and the formula to convert the 16-bit value to percentage humidity is:

```
RH= -6 + 125 * data16 / 2^16
```

This can be implemented in integer arithmetic if we work with RH*100. Putting all this together and reusing some variables from the previous program we have:

```
buf[0]=0xE5;
uBit.i2c.write(0x80, buf, 1);
uBit.i2c.read(0x80, buf, 3);
msb = buf[0];
lsb = buf[1];
check = buf[2];
printf("\n\rmsb %d \n\rlsb %d \n\rchecksum %d \n\r",
                                msb, lsb, check);
data16 = ((unsigned int) msb << 8) | (unsigned int) (lsb & 0xFC);
int hum=-600+((12500*data16)>>16);
printf("Humidity %d.%d %% \n\r", hum / 100, hum % 100);
```

The only unusual part of the program is using %% to print a single % character - necessary because % means something in printf.

## Checksum calculation

Although computing a checksum isn't specific to I2C, it is another common task. The datasheet explains that the polynomial used is:

$$X8 + X5 + X4 + 1$$

Once you have this information you can work out the divisor by writing a binary number with a one in each location corresponding to a power of X in the polynomial, i.e. the 8th, 5th, 4th and 1st bit. Hence the divisor is 0x0131.

What you do next is roughly the same for all CRCs. First you put the data that was used to compute the checksum together with the checksum value as the low order bits:

```
uint32_t data32 = ((uint32_t)msb << 16)|
((uint32_t) lsb <<8) |(uint32_t) check;
```

Now you have three bytes, i.e 24 bits, in a 32-bit variable.

Next you adjust the divisor so that its most significant non-zero bit aligns with the most significant bit of the three bytes. As this divisor has a one at bit eight it needs to be shifted 15 places to the right to move it to be the 24th bit:

```
uint32_t divisor = ((uint32_t) 0x0131) <<15;
```

Now that you have both the data and the divisor aligned, you step through the top-most 16 bits, i.e. you don't process the low order eight bits which is the received checksum. For each bit you check to see if it is a one - if it is you replace the data with the data XOR divisor. In either case you shift the divisor one place to the right:

```
for (int i = 0 ; i < 16 ; i++){
 if( data32 & (uint32_t)1<<(23 -i))data32 =data32 ^ divisor;
 divisor=divisor >> 1;
};
```

When the loop ends, if there was no error, the data32 should be zeroed and the received checksum is correct and as computed on the data received.

A complete function to compute the checksum with some optimizations is:

```
uint8_t crcCheck(uint8_t msb, uint8_t lsb, uint8_t check){
uint32_t data32 =((uint32_t)msb << 16)|
                    ((uint32_t)lsb <<8)|(uint32_t) check;
uint32_t divisor = 0x988000;
for (int i = 0 ; i < 16 ; i++){
  if( data32 & (uint32_t)1<<(23 - i) )data32 ^= divisor;
  divisor>>= 1;
 };
 return (uint8_t) data32;
}
```

It is rare to get a crc error on an I2C bus unless it is overloaded or subject to a lot of noise.

## Another Bus

If you don't want to use the internal I2C bus then you have to give over two additional GPIO lines to the task of implementing a second one. If you need to do this then the good news is that it is fairly easy because the framework takes care of everything, including configuring the GPIO lines to be open collector.

All you have to do is instantiate your own I2C object - remembering not to instantiate or use a uBit object and making sure the all the objects you create are global.

If you want to convert the program that we have developed so far you also need a serial object to make printf send its results to the serial port:

```
MicroBitI2C i2c(PAD1, PAD2);
MicroBitSerial serial(USBTX, USBRX);
```

In this case the I2C lines have been allocated to the first two PADs, i.e. Pin 0 and Pin 1 on the edge connector. If you do this then you have to make sure that you don't configure or attempt to use these GPIO lines for any other purpose.

With this change, all we have to do is connect the HTU21D SDA and SCL lines to Pin 0 and Pin 1 and change the program to use the i2c and serial objects

```
int main() {
    char buf[4] = {0xE3};
    i2c.write(0x80, buf, 1);
    i2c.read(0x80, buf, 3);
    uint8_t msb = buf[0];
    uint8_t lsb = buf[1];
    uint8_t check = buf[2];

    serial.printf("\n\rmsb %d \n\rlsb %d \n\rchecksum %d \n\r",
                                        msb, lsb, check);
    serial.printf("crc %d \n ", crcCheck(msb,lsb,check));

    unsigned int data16 = ((unsigned int) msb << 8) |
                            (unsigned int) (lsb & 0xFC);
    int temp = -4685 + ((17572 * data16) >> 16);
    serial.printf("Temperature %d.%d C \n\r",
                            temp / 100, temp % 100);
```

You can make the same changes to the rest of the program.

# Complete Listing

The complete program including crc checks is:

```c
#include "MicroBit.h"
MicroBit uBit;
uint8_t crcCheck(uint8_t msb, uint8_t lsb, uint8_t check);

int main() {
    uBit.init();

    char buf[4] = {0xE3};
    uBit.i2c.write(0x80, buf, 1);
    uBit.i2c.read(0x80, buf, 3);
    uint8_t msb = buf[0];
    uint8_t lsb = buf[1];
    uint8_t check = buf[2];

    printf("\n\rmsb %d \n\rlsb %d \n\rchecksum %d \n\r",
                                        msb, lsb, check);
    printf("crc %d \n ", crcCheck(msb,lsb,check));

    unsigned int data16 = ((unsigned int) msb << 8) |
                            (unsigned int) (lsb & 0xFC);
    int temp = -4685 + ((17572 * data16) >> 16);
    printf("Temperature %d.%d C \n\r", temp / 100, temp % 100);

    buf[0] = 0xE5;
    uBit.i2c.write(0x80, buf, 1);
    uBit.i2c.read(0x80, buf, 3);
    msb = buf[0];
    lsb = buf[1];
    check = buf[2];
    printf("\n\rmsb %d \n\rlsb %d \n\rchecksum %d \n\r",
                                        msb, lsb, check);
    printf("crc %d \n ", crcCheck(msb,lsb,check));

    data16 = ((unsigned int) msb << 8) |
                    (unsigned int) (lsb & 0xFC);
    int hum = -600 + ((12500 * data16) >> 16);
    printf("Humidity %d.%d %% \n\r", hum / 100, hum % 100);

    uint32_t data32 = ((uint32_t) msb << 16) |
                    ((uint32_t) lsb << 8) | (uint32_t) check;

    release_fiber();
    return 0;
}
```

```
uint8_t crcCheck(uint8_t msb, uint8_t lsb, uint8_t check) {
    uint32_t data32 = ((uint32_t) msb << 16)|
                      ((uint32_t) lsb << 8) | (uint32_t) check;
    uint32_t divisor = 0x988000;
    for (int i = 0; i < 16; i++) {
        if (data32 & (uint32_t) 1 << (23 - i))
            data32 ^= divisor;
        divisor >>= 1;
    };
    return (uint8_t) data32;
}
```

Of course this is just the start. Once you have the device working and supplying data it is time to write your code in the form of functions that return the temperature and the humidity and generally make the whole thing more useful and easier to maintain.

This is often how this sort of programming goes. At first you write a lot of inline code so that it works as fast as it can, then you move blocks of code to functions to make the program more elegant and easy to maintain, checking at each refactoring that the programming still works.

Not all devices used standard bus protocols. Next we looks at a custom serial protocol that we have to implement for ourselves.

# Chapter 8
# A Custom Protocol DHT11/DHT22

In this chapter we make use of all the ideas introduced in earlier chapters to create a raw interface with the low cost DHT11/22 temperature and humidity sensor as an exercise in implementing a custom protocol directly in C.

## The DHT22

The DHT22 is a more accurate version of the DHT11 and it is used in this project, but the hardware and software will work with both version and with the AM2302 which is similar to the DHT22.

```
Model AM2302/DHT22
Power supply 3.3-5.5V DC
Output signal digital signal via 1-wire bus
Sensing element Polymer humidity capacitor
Operating range
  humidity 0-100%RH;
  temperature -40~80Celsius
Accuracy
  humidity +-2%RH(Max +-5%RH);
  temperature +-0.5Celsius
Resolution or sensitivity
  humidity 0.1%RH;
  temperature 0.1Celsius
Repeatability
  humidity +-1%RH;
  temperature +-0.2Celsius
```

The device will work at 3.3V and it makes use of a 1-wire open collector style bus, which makes it very easy to make the physical connection to the micro:bit. The one-wire bus used isn't standard and is only used by this family of devices so we have little choice but to implement the protocol in C.

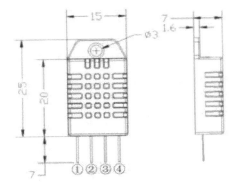

The pinouts are:

1. VDD
2. SDA serial data
3. not used
4. GND

and the standard way of connecting the device is:

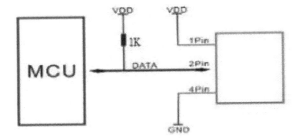

Although the recommended pull up resistor is 1K, a higher value works better with the micro:bit - typically 4.7K, but larger will work.

The serial protocol is fairly simple. The host pulls the line low for between 0.8 and 29 ms, usually 1ms. It then releases the bus which is pulled high. After 20 to 200 microseconds, usually 30 microseconds, the device starts to send data by pulling the line down for around 80 microseconds and then lets it float high for another 80 microseconds. Next 40 bits of data are sent using a 70 microsecond high for a 1 and a 26 microsecond high for a 0 with the high pulses separated by around 50 microsecond low periods.

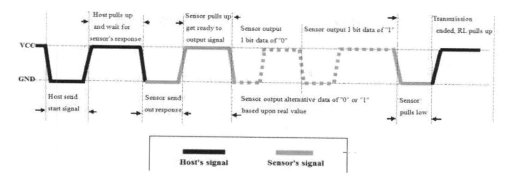

So what we have to do is pull the line low for 1ms or so to start the device sending data and this is very easy. Then we have to wait for the device to pull the line down and let it pull up again for about 160 microsecond and then read the time that the line is high 80 times.

A 1 corresponds to 70 microseconds and a 0 corresponds to 26 microseconds. This is within the range of pulse measurement that can be achieved using standard library function. There is also a 50-microsecond period between each data bit and this can be used to do some limited processing. Notice that we are only interested in the time that the line is held high.

## The Electronics

Exactly how you build the circuit is a matter of preference. The basic layout can be seen below:

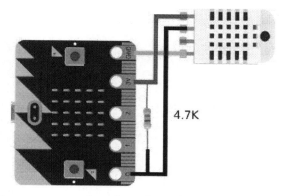

If you have an edge connector breakout board for the micro:bit then it is fairly easy to connect the device to the micro:bit using female jumper wires.

You can also put the resistor close to the DHT22 to make a sensor package connected to the micro:bit using three cables.

# The Software

With the hardware shown above connected to the micro:bit the first thing that we need to do is establish that the system is working - just a little.

The simplest way to do this is to pull the line down for 1ms and see if the device responds with a stream of pulses. These can be seen on a logic analyzer or an oscilloscope - both are indispensable tools.

If you don't have access to either tool then you will just have to skip to the next stage and see if you can read in some data.

The simplest program that will do the job is:

```
#include "MicroBit.h"
MicroBit uBit;
MicroBitPin P0=uBit.io.P0;;
 int main() {
 uBit.init();
 P0.setDigitalValue(1);
 P0.setDigitalValue(0);
 volatile int i;
 for (i = 0; i < 1200; i++) {
 };
 int b = P0.getDigitalValue();
}
```

Setting the line initially high, to ensure that it is configured as an output, we then set it low, wait for around 1000 microseconds and then change its direction to input by reading the data.

There is no need to set the lines pull up mode because it is the only device driving the line until it releases the line by changing direction to input. When a line is in input mode it is high impedance and this is why we need an external pull up resistor in the circuit.

As long as the circuit has been correctly assembled and you have a working device you should see something like:

# Reading the Data

With preliminary flight checks complete it is time to read the 40-bit data stream. The first thing to do is wait for the low that the device sends before the START bit:

```
for (i = 1; i < 200; i++) {
  if (P0.getDigitalValue() == 0)break;
};
```

Next we can start to read in the bit stream. When doing this there are two things to keep in mind. The first is that it is only the time the line is high that matters and you need to measure this accurately - you don't care so much about how long the line is low for.

The second is that it is usually better to collect the bits and only later process them and extract the data. To this end it is usually a good idea to save the data in a buffer.

```
int buf[41];
int j;
 for(j=0;j<41;j++){
  for(i=1;i<200;i++){
   if(P0.getDigitalValue()==1)break;
  };
  for(i=1;i<200;i++){
   if(P0.getDigitalValue()==0) break;
  }
  buf[j]=i;
}
```

You should be able to see how this works. The outer for loop, indexed on j, repeats to read in all 41 bits, 40 data bits and the initial START bit. The first inner loop waits for the line to go high and i gives the time that the line has been low. This is of no interest because the device keeps the line low for the same length of time for a zero or a one. Next the second for loop waits for the line to go low. The count in i is now proportional to the time the line was high and is stored in the buffer.

If you add:

```
for(j=0;j<=40;j++){
 printf("%d %d \n",j,buf[j]);
}
```

to the end of the program you will be able to see the counts and you should quickly be able to work out the value half way between the long one pulses and the short zero pulses.

To see the output you have to install the mbed USB serial driver and use a serial terminal like PuTTy. Examining the data reveals that short pulses returned 6 and long returned 16 both plus or minus 1. Thus the threshold is approximately 11.

With a threshold of 11 we can classify the pulses into long and short and store 1s and 0s in the buffer.

```
int buf[41];
int j;
for (j = 0; j < 41; j++) {
  for (i = 1; i < 200; i++) {
    if (P0.getDigitalValue() == 1)break;
  };
  for (i = 1; i < 200; i++) {
    if (P0.getDigitalValue() == 0) break;
  }
  buf[j] = 0;
  if (i > 11)buf[j] = 1;
}
```

You can afford to include this extra processing in the data collection loop because it happens while the line is low and we aren't interested in measuring this time accurately.

**If you try this out you will discover that it doesn't work.** You will discover that it drops bits and its seems to drop the same bits each time you run the program. This suggests that it is a systematic effect and not the result of random noise. The cause of the problem is the system timer interrupt. The entire transaction takes about one timer interrupt interval and as the timer is stated when the program starts the interrupt occurs at the same point each time you run the program - hence the regularity.

**What can be done?** The most obvious thing to do is switch the timer off but there is a simpler solution. All you have to do is include a call to the sleep function just before you start the transaction. When sleep returns a timer event must have just occurred and you have a little less than 6ms of uninterrupted processing - which is just enough. As we have to use a 1ms sleep we might as well put the call into the initiation pulse and remove the for loop:

```
int main() {
    uBit.init();
    P0.setDigitalValue(1);
    P0.setDigitalValue(0)
    volatile int i;
    uBit.sleep(1);
    P0.getDigitalValue();
```

With this change the program works perfectly.

# Extracting the Data

Now we have the data in the buffer as zeros and ones. All that remains is to decode it into temperature and humidity readings. But first we will convert the bits into five bytes of data.

The simplest way of doing this is to write a function that will pack eight bits into an uint:

```
uint getByte(int b,int buf[]){
  int i;
  uint result=0;
  b=(b-1)*8+1;
  for(i=b;i<=b+7;i++){
    result= result<<1;
    result=result | buf[i];
  }
  return result;
}
```

The b can be set to the byte that you want to extract from the array. For example, if b=2 then the for loop runs from i=9 to i=16 i.e. the second byte stored in the array. Notice that we skip the first bit because this just signals the start of the data. The bit manipulation in the for loop is a fairly standard shift left and or the least significant bit into the result.

Using this function getting the five bytes is trivial:

```
uint byte1=getByte(1,buf);
uint byte2=getByte(2,buf);
uint byte3=getByte(3,buf);
uint byte4=getByte(4,buf);
uint byte5=getByte(5,buf);
```

The first two bytes are the humidity measurement, the second two the temperature and the final byte is the checksum. The checksum is just the sum of the first four bytes reduced to eight bits and we can test it using:

```
printf("Checksum %d %d \n",byte5,byte1+byte2+byte3+byte4) & 0xFF);
```

If the two values are different there has been a transmission error.

In this case the simplest thing to do is get another reading from the device. However notice that you shouldn't read the device more than once every 2 seconds.

The humidity and temperature data are also easy to reconstruct as they are transmitted high byte first and times 10 the actual value.

The only problem is that the micro:bit doesn't have hardware floating point support and so it is easier to keep the values as humidity*10 and temperature*10.

The humidity data is easy:

```
int16_t humidity = (byte1 << 8) | byte2;
```

The temperature data is slightly more difficult in that the top most bit is used to indicate a negative temperature. This isn't two's complement or any other standard format. The most significant bit is simply used as a negative sign for the value stored as a positive binary value in the lower order bits.

This means we have to test for the most significant bit and flip the sign of the temperature if it is set:

```
int16_t temperature = (byte3 << 8) | byte4;
if(temperature & 0x8000)temperature=-(temperature & 0x7FFF);
```

This completes the data processing all that is left is showing the data to the user.

For testing it is good to send the data to the serial port so that it can be checked:

```
printf("Checksum %X %X \n\r",
            byte5, (byte1 + byte2 + byte3 + byte4) & 0xFF);
printf("Humidity %hd.%hd%%\n\r",
            humidity / 10, abs(humidity % 10));
printf("Temperature %hd.%hdC\n\r",
            temperature / 10, abs(temperature % 10));
```

The only unusual features of the printf statements are the use of %% to display a percentage sign and the use of %hd to format a short integer. Notice that the format strings print the humidity as dd.d% and the temperature as dd.dC.

As the micro:bit also has a 5x5 LED display why not use it to show the humidity and temperature:

```
char buff[10];
sprintf(buff, "%hd.%hd%%",
            humidity / 10, abs(humidity % 10));
uBit.display.scroll(buff, 200);
sprintf(buff, "%hd.%hdC",
            temperature / 10, abs(temperature % 10));
uBit.display.scroll(buff, 200);
```

Now if you run the program you will see the humidity and temperature scroll past. If you put the whole reading section into a loop then you can add a uBit.sleep(2500) to produce something that shows the data every 2.5 seconds.

## Complete Listing

That's all we need to do and the final program, complete with some minor tidying up, can be seen below:

```
#include "MicroBit.h"
uint getByte(int, int[]);
MicroBit uBit;
MicroBitPin P0 = uBit.io.P0;

int main() {
    uBit.init();
    P0.setDigitalValue(1);
    for(;;){
     P0.setDigitalValue(0);
     volatile int i;
     uBit.sleep(1);
     P0.getDigitalValue();
     for (i = 1; i < 200; i++) {
       if (P0.getDigitalValue() == 0)break;
     };
     int buf[41];
     int j;
     for (j = 0; j < 41; j++) {
         for (i = 1; i < 200; i++) {
             if (P0.getDigitalValue() == 1)break;
         };
         for (i = 1; i < 200; i++) {
             if (P0.getDigitalValue() == 0) break;
         }
         buf[j] = 0;
         if (i > 11)buf[j] = 1;
     }
    uint byte1 = getByte(1, buf);
    uint byte2 = getByte(2, buf);
    uint byte3 = getByte(3, buf);
    uint byte4 = getByte(4, buf);
    uint byte5 = getByte(5, buf);

    int16_t humidity = (byte1 << 8) | byte2;
    int16_t temperature = (byte3 << 8) | byte4;
    if(temperature & 0x8000)
            temperature=-(temperature & 0x7FFF);
```

```
        printf("Checksum %X %X \n\r",
                byte5, (byte1 + byte2 + byte3 + byte4) & 0xFF);
        printf("Humidity %hd.%hd%%\n\r",
                humidity / 10, abs(humidity % 10));
        printf("Temperature %hd.%hdC\n\r",
                temperature / 10, abs(temperature % 10));
        char buff[10];
        sprintf(buff,"%hd.%hd%%",humidity / 10, abs(humidity % 10));
        uBit.display.scroll(buff, 200);
        sprintf(buff,"%hd.%hdC",temperature / 10, abs(temperature%10));
        uBit.display.scroll(buff, 200);
        uBit.sleep(2500);
    }
}

uint getByte(int b, int buf[]) {
    int i;
    uint result = 0;
    b = (b - 1)*8 + 1;
    for (i = b; i <= b + 7; i++) {
        result = result << 1;
        result = result | buf[i];
    }
    return result;
}
```

Obviously the code needs to be refactored into a function that accepts the pin to which the device is connected and returns humidity and temperature.

The DHT11/22 is a useful device but when it comes to low cost temperature measurement the DS18D20 is a very popular choice and is more accurate than the DHT11/22. This is the subject of the next chapter.

# Chapter 9
# DS18B20 1-Wire Temperature Sensor

The Maxim 1-Wire bus is a proprietary bus that is very easy to use and has a lot of useful devices you can connect to it, including the iButton security devices. Probably the most popular of all 1-wire devices is the DS18B20 temperature sensor - it is small, very cheap and very easy to use **if** the processor supports the 1-wire bus protocol and the micro:bit doesn't. However, the protocol is easy enough to program in C and the micro:bit is fast enough to work with it without needing anything extra. Of course, we have to work in C; Python, for example, just isn't fast enough.

The micro:bit does have an onboard temperature sensor, but this measures the temperature of the CPU and only gives you the air temperature very approximately. The DS18B20 gives you an accurate temperature and you can have multiple sensors.

## The Hardware

The DS18B20 is available in an number of formats but the most common makes it look just like a standard BJT - which can sometimes be a problem when you are trying to find one.

You can also get them made up into waterproof sensors complete with cable.

No matter how packaged, they will work at 3.3V or 5V.

The basic specification of the DS18B20 is:

- Measures Temperatures from -55°C to +125°C (-67°F to +257°F)
- ±0.5°C Accuracy from -10°C to +85°C
- Thermometer Resolution is User Selectable from 9 to 12 Bits
- Converts Temperature to 12-Bit Digital Word in 750ms (Max)

It can also be powered from the data line making the bus physically need only two wires - data and ground - however this "parasitic power" mode is difficult to make work reliably and best avoided in an initial design.

In normal powered mode there are just three connections:

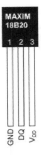

Ground needs to be connected to the system ground, VDD to 3.3V and DQ to the pull-up resistor of an open collector bus.

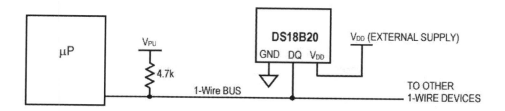

There can be multiple devices on the bus and each one has a unique 64-bit lasered ROM code, which can be used as an address to select the active devices. For simplicity, it is better to start off with a single device and avoid the problem of enumerating the devices on the bus - although once you know how everything works this isn't difficult to implement.

There is a problem we have to solve, however, the need for fast switching between input and output. Without intervention, changing between output and input mode is done using the system and is comparatively slow, approximately 80 microseconds. In some cases this does matter because the protocol requires data from the master and then receives data from the slave. For example, the DHT22 temperature and humidity sensor asks the processor to write to it to start a measurement and then sends data back without the processor writing anything else. In this case we could use a single GPIO line, send the data, switch to input and read the data.

In the case of the 1-wire bus things are very different. The master has to send a fast pulse on the line for every bit received and it has to be able to read the response in around 15 microseconds. This is too fast to allow for the line to change from output to input in time to read the data although it could be done by writing directly to the GPIO registers.

A secure and simple solution that should work with all 1-wire bus devices is to use two GPIO lines - one set to output and one set to input. If you can't afford to use two GPIO lines then there is a way to do the job with one, but only by resorting to directly accessing the GPIO line and not using the mbed library functions, see the end of this chapter for more details.

You can use any pair of GPIO lines, but for simplicity this example uses P0 and P1. The DS18B20 can be directly connected to the micro:bit's PADs. The only complication is that you do need the pullup resistor. The internal pullup resistor is around 10K to 15K and is just too large to work. You need to put a 4.7K resistor in parallel with it to decrease the resistance.

The circuit is:

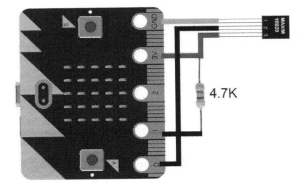

You can build it in a variety of ways. You could solder the resistor to the temperature sensor and then use some longer wires with clips to connect to the micro:bit. You could also solder directly to the micro:bit or use a prototyping board.

## Initialization

Every transaction with the a 1-wire device starts with an initialization handshake. First we have to get the GPIO lines set up correctly:

```
MicroBit uBit;
MicroBitPin P0=uBit.io.P0;;
MicroBitPin P1= uBit.io.P1;

int main() {
 uBit.init();
 P0.setDigitalValue(1);
 P0.setPull(PullUp);
 P1.getDigitalValue();
```

We have the usual initialization of the MicroBit object and for simplicity we define P0 and P1 as short cuts to the pins we are using. P0 is initialized by setting it to output a 1 and P1 is read, just to set it to input. This gets both pins ready so that the first read/write doesn't waste time configuring I/O direction.

The only out of the ordinary part of the initialization is the use of setPull. This configures and output pin to be one of:

- PullNone - standard pushpull output
- PullDown - pull down with a 10-15K resistor
- PullUp - pull up with a 10-10K resistor

If you try to enter setPull and it isn't recognized then the chances are you are using an early version of the library as setPull was introduced in RC3. You can't update the library manually if you are using the online compiler. If you are using the off line approach using yotta or NetBeans then use yotta uninstall to remove the microbit module and then reinstall it using yotta install:

```
yotta uninstall microbit
yotta install lancaster-university/microbit
```

It is also a good idea to delete the module files before re-installing them. Delete everything in the folder yotta_modules and then use the install command.

If after this NetBeans still cannot locate setPull use the command Tools,Options, select the C/C++ tab, then the Code Assistance tab and add the include directory that corresponds to yotta_modules\microbit-dal\inc.

Now we have to send the initialization pulse. This is simply a low pulse that lasts at least 480 microseconds, a 15 to 60 microsecond pause follows and then any devices on the bus pull the line low for 60 to 240 microseconds.

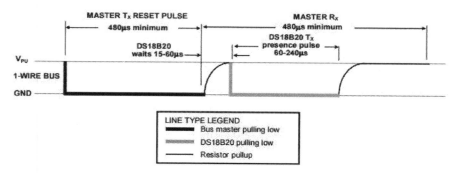

This is fairly easy to implement as a function:

```
int init() {
 volatile int i;
 P0.setDigitalValue(0);
 for (i = 0; i < 600; i++) {};
 P0.setDigitalValue(1);
 for (i = 0;i < 30;i++) {};
 int b = P1.getDigitalValue();
 for (i = 0;i < 600;i++) {};
 return b;
}
```

Notice that the index of the for loop has to be declared as volatile to stop the compiler from optimizing the code by removing the null loop completely.

We pull the line low for 500 microseconds and then let it be pulled back up. After a 30-microsecond wait, which is right at the start of the guaranteed period when the line should be low, if there is an active device on the bus we read the input line and then wait another 500 microseconds to complete the data slot. The timings in this case are not critical as long as the P1 line is read while it is held low by the slaves - which is never less than 60 microseconds and is typically as much as 100 microseconds. The actual pulse timings with the values given are 530 microsecond reset, 31 microsecond pause and a 450 microsecond final part of the data slot.

If there is a device the function should return 0 and if there are no devices it should return 1:

```
if(init()==1){
 printf("No device \n");
}
```

If you try this partial program using a logic analyzer with a 1-wire protocol analyzer you will see something like:

Seeing a presence pulse is the simplest and quickest way to be sure that your hardware is working.

## Writing Bits

Our next task is to implement the sending of some data bits to the device.

The 1-wire bus has a very simple data protocol. All bits are sent using a minimum of 60 microseconds for a read/write slot. Each slot must be separated from the next by a minimum of 1 microsecond.

The good news is that timing is only critical within each slot. You can send the first bit in a time slot and then take your time before you send the next bit, the device will wait for you. This means you only have to worry about timing within the functions that read and write individual bits.

To send a 0 you have to hold the line low for most of the slot.

To send a 1 you have to hold the line low for between 1 and 15 microseconds and leave the line high for the rest of the slot.

The exact timings can be seen below:

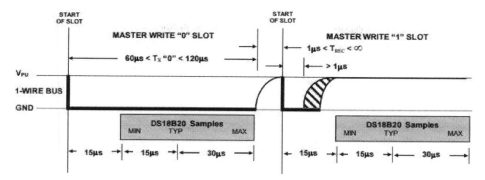

It seems reasonable to use the typical timings shown on the diagram.

So for a 0 we hold the line low for 60 microsecond then let it go high for the remainder of the slot.

To send a 1 we hold the line for a bit more than 1 microsecond and then let it go high for the remainder of the slot.

The sendZero function is:

```
void sendZero() {
 volatile int i;
 P0.setDigitalValue(0);
 for (i = 1; i < 75; i++) {};
 P0.setDigitalValue(1);
 for (i = 1; i < 6; i++) {};
}
```

The sendOne function is:

```
void sendOne() {
 volatile int i;
 P0.setDigitalValue(0);
 for (i = 1; i < 1; i++) {};
 P0.setDigitalValue(1);
 for (i = 1; i < 80; i++) {};
}
```

Notice that the functions keep control after letting the line go high again. In principle they could return and let the main program do some processing, but this would mean that the main program had to hold off sending another bit until the 60 microseconds was up. This approach isn't efficient, but it is simple. Also notice that, as the time periods are short and have to be fairly repeatable, a busy wait is the best option for the delay.

With these constants the measured pulse widths are:

For a 0 the the line is held low for just about 60 microseconds with a pause of about 10 microseconds.

For a 1 the line is held low for 4 microseconds and the slot is about 70 microseconds in total.

As the only time critical operations are the actual setting of the line low and then back to high, there is no need to worry too much about speed of operation of the entire function so we might as well combine the two functions into a single writeBit function:

```
void writeBit(int b) {
 volatile int i;
 int delay1, delay2;
 if (b == 1) {
  delay1 = 1;
  delay2 = 80;
 } else {
  delay1 = 75;
  delay2 = 6;
 }
 P0.setDigitalValue(0);
 for (i = 1; i < delay1; i++) {};
 P0.setDigitalValue(1);
 for (i = 1; i < delay2; i++) {};
}
```

The code at the start of the function simply increases the time between slots slightly.

You can see a one followed by a zero in the following logic analyzer trace:

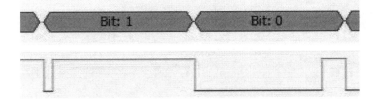

120

# A First Command

After discovering that there is at least one device connected to the bus, the master has to issue a ROM command. In many cases the ROM command used first will be the Search ROM command which enumerates the 64-bit codes of all of the devices on the bus. After collecting all of these codes the master can use Match ROM commands with a specific 64-bit code to select the device the master wants to talk to.

While it is perfectly possible to implement the Search ROM procedure, it is simpler to work with the single device by using commands which ignore the 64-bit code and address all of the devices on the bus at the same time. Of course, this only works as long as there is only one device on the bus.

If there is only one device then we can use the Skip ROM command, 0xCC, to tell all the devices on the bus to be active.

As we have a writeBit function this is easy:

```
void sendskip(){
 writeBit(0);
 writeBit(0);
 writeBit(1);
 writeBit(1);
 writeBit(0);
 writeBit(0);
 writeBit(1);
 writeBit(1);
}
```

Notice that 0xCC is 1100 1100 in binary and the 1-wire bus sends the least significant bit first. If you try this out you should find it works but device doesn't respond because it is waiting for another command.

Again as the time between writing bits isn't critical we can take this first implementation of the function and write something more general if slightly slower.

The writeByte function will write the low 8 bits of an int to the device:

```
void writeByte(int byte){
int i;
 for(i=0;i<8;i++){
  if(byte & 1){
   writeBit(1);
  }else{
   writeBit(0);
  }
  byte=byte>>1;
 }
}
```

Using this we can send a Skip ROM command using:

```
writeByte(0xCC);
```

You can see the pattern of bits sent on a logic analyzer:

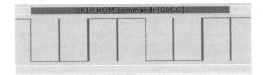

## Reading Bits

We already know how the master sends a 1 and a 0. The protocol for the slave device is exactly the same except that the master still provides the slot's starting pulse. That is, the master starts a 60-microsecond slot by pulling the bus down for a bit more than 1 microsecond. Then the slave device either holds the line down for a further 15 microseconds minimum or it simply allows the line to float high. See below for the exact timings:

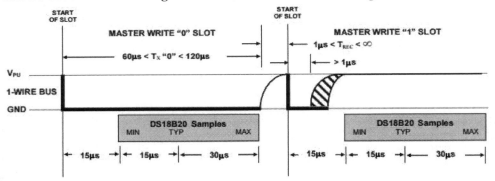

So all we have to do to read bits is to pull the line down for just a bit more than 1 microsecond and then sample the bus at the end of a 15 microsecond pause:

```
int readBit() {
 volatile int i;
 P0.setDigitalValue(0);
 P0.setDigitalValue(1);
 for (i = 1; i < 20; i++) {};
 int b = P1.getDigitalValue();
 for (i = 1; i < 60; i++) {};
 return b;
}
```

The readBit function pulls the line low for about 4 microsecond and measures the line state at around 15 microseconds. The total slot time is around 70 microseconds. Again it is better to use busy waits as the time periods are short and need to be repeatable.

A logic analyzer shows the typical pattern of bits from the device:

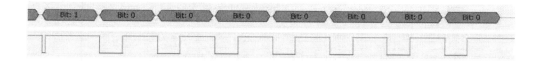

## Initiating A Temperature Conversion

Our next task is to send a Convert command, 0x44. This starts the DS18B20 making a temperature measurement. Depending on the resolution selected this can take as long as 750ms. How the device tells the master that the measurement has completed depends on the mode it is operating in, but using an external power line, i.e. not using parasitic mode, the device sends a 0 bit in response to a bit read until it is completed when it sends a 1.

As we already have a readBit function this is easy. The software polls for the completion by reading the bus until it gets a 1 bit:

```
int convert() {
  volatile int i;
  int j;
  writeByte(0x44);
  for (j = 1; j < 1000; j++) {
   for (i = 1; i < 900; i++) {};
   if (readBit() == 1)break;
  };
  return (j);
}
```

You can of course test the return value to check that the result has been obtained. When the function returns, the new temperature measurement is stored in the device's scratchpad memory and now all we have to do is read this.

## Reading the Scratchpad

The scratchpad memory has nine bytes of storage in total and does things like control the accuracy of conversion and provide status information. However in our simple example the only two bytes of any great interest are the first two - which hold the result of a temperature conversion.

Before we move on to read the scratchpad we need a function that will read a byte. As in the case of writing a byte there is no time criticality in the time between reading bits so we don't need to take extra special care in constructing the function;

```
int readByte(){
 int byte=0;
 int i;
 for(i=0;i<8;i++){
  byte=byte | readBit()<< i;
 };
 return byte;
}
```

The only difficult part is to remember that the 1-wire bus sends the least significant bit first and so this has to be shifted into the result from the right.

Now we have a readByte function getting the data is simple. We have to issue a Read Scratchpad 0xBE command and then read the nine bytes that the device returns. However, to send the new command we have to issue a new initialization pulse and a Skip ROM 0xCC command followed by a read scratchpad command 0xBE:

```
init(); writeByte(0xCC);
writeByte(0xBE);
```

Now the data is ready to read and we can read all nine bytes of it or just the first two. The device will keep track of where the read is, so if you come back later and read more bytes you will get the first one not read. If you issue an initialization pulse then the device aborts the data transmission.

We only need the first two bytes, which are the least and most significant bytes of the 11-bit temperature reading as a 16-bit, 2-complement integer.

```
int b1= readByte();
int b2= readByte();
```

## Getting the Temperature

All we now have to do do is to put the two bytes together as a 16-bit integer. As the micro:bit supports a 16-bit int we can do this very easily:

```
int16_t temp1= (b2<<8 | b1) ;
```

Finally we need to convert this to a floating point value. As already discussed, the micro:bit doesn't support this in hardware. As all we really want is two digits to give the tens and two digits to give the fractional part it is easier to work in integer arithmetic using temperature*100:

```
temp = temp * 100 / 16;
```

This gives us an integer value that represents the temperature in hundredths of a degree centigrade, e.g. 25.45C is represented as 2545. Notice that this only works because int16_t really is a 16-bit integer. If you were to use a 32-bit int:

```
int temp1= (b2<<8 | b1);
```

then temp1 would be correct for positive temperatures but it would give the wrong answer for negative values because the sign bit isn't propagated into the top 16 bits. So if using a 32-bit integer, propagate the sign bit manually:

```
int temp1=(b2<<8 | b1);
if(b2 & 0x80) temp1=temp1 | 0xFFFF0000;
```

Assuming we have the temperature in 100ths in temp, we can now display it on the micro:bit's LED matrix. First we need to convert it into a string:

```
char buff[10];
sprintf(buff, "%d.%d", temp / 100, abs(temp % 100));
```

Now we can display the string:

```
uBit.display.scroll(buff, 200);
```

That finalizes a basic program to read the temperature and create some useful 1-wire functions. The next task would be to refactor more of the code to create a function that reads the temperature on demand.

## Using a Single GPIO Line

The library just isn't fast enough to change the direction of a GPIO line and read the state and switch back to output again in time to read the pulse sent by the slave device.

If you make use of direct access to the GPIO control registers, however, this can be done. The details of how the GPIO registers work are in Chapter 4.

The only function that we need to change is the readBit function. First we need to set up some addresses:

```
volatile unsigned int *setdir =(unsigned int *)(0x50000000UL+0x518);
volatile unsigned int *clrdir =(unsigned int *)(0x50000000UL+0x51C);
volatile unsigned int *inp =(unsigned int *)(0x50000000UL+0x510);
uint32_t mask = 1 << 3;
```

The **setdir** and **clrdir** registers set the line to output and input respectively. That is, writing a 1 to a location in setdir sets the corresponding pin to output and writing a 1 to the same location in clrdir sets that corresponding pin to input. Notice that writing zeros to any location in either register has no effect. The **inp** register can be read to get the state of all the input lines in the GPIO.

The pin that we want to work with is P0, which maps to nRF51's GPIO PIN3, the third bit in the register, hence mask=4 or 100 in binary. In general the mask for pin n is 1<<n.

Now all we have to do is modify the readBit function to use the same GPIO line to read the data. All we have to do is change the GPIO lines direction to input, read it and then set it back to output.

```
int readBit() {
 volatile int i;
 P0.setDigitalValue(0);
 P0.setDigitalValue(1);
 for (i = 1;i < 20;i++) {}
 *clrdir = mask;
 unsigned int b = (*inp) & mask;
 b = b >> 3;
 *setdir = mask;
 for (i = 1;i < 60;i++) {};
 return b;
}
```

Notice that we use the library functions to generate the microsecond pulse that starts the read. Next comes a short pause and then we change the direction by writing the mask to the clrdir register, read the state of the line and and it with the mask to just get the third bit which corresponds to P0. To return a 1 is the third bit is set we simply shift 3 places right. Finally we return P0 to output by writing the mask to the setdir register.

With this version of the readBit function you should find that everything works as before.

Once you have the basic bit read/write functions the rest follows fairly easily. Missing from the program given below is the ability to write to the configuration register to select the resolution, but in most cases the 12-bit default is what you want. Also missing is the CRC calculation to check for errors and most important of all the enumeration algorithm that discovers what 1-wire devices are active on the bus. All the omissions are fairly straightforward to provide now that we have the low-level data functions.

You can also expand the operation to other 1-wire devices such as iButtons etc.

## Complete Listing

```c
#include "MicroBit.h"

int init();
void sendskip();
void writeBit(int);
void sendOne();
void sendZero();
void writeByte(int);
int readBit();
int convert();
int readByte();

MicroBit uBit;

MicroBitPin P0 = uBit.io.P0;
MicroBitPin P1 = uBit.io.P1;

int main() {
 uBit.init();

 P0.setDigitalValue(1);
 P0.setPull(PullUp);
 P1.getDigitalValue();
 uBit.sleep(1);
 while (1) {
  init();
  writeByte(0xCC);
  int r = convert();
  init();
  writeByte(0xCC);
  writeByte(0xBE);
  int b1 = readByte();
  int b2 = readByte();
  int16_t temp = (b2 << 8 | b1);  temp = temp * 100 / 16;
  char buff[10];
  sprintf(buff, "%d.%d", temp / 100, abs(temp % 100));
  uBit.display.scroll(buff, 200);
  uBit.sleep(1000);
 }
 release_fiber();
}
```

```
int init() {
 volatile int i;P0.setDigitalValue(0);
 for (i = 0; i < 600; i++) {};
 P0.setDigitalValue(1);
 for (i = 0; i < 30; i++) {};
 int b = P1.getDigitalValue();
 for (i = 0; i < 600; i++) {};
 return b;
}

void sendZero() {
 volatile int i;
 P0.setDigitalValue(0);
 for (i = 1; i < 75; i++) {};
 P0.setDigitalValue(1);
 for (i = 1; i < 6; i++) {};
}

void sendOne() {
 volatile int i;
 P0.setDigitalValue(0);
 for (i = 1; i < 1; i++) {};
 P0.setDigitalValue(1);
 for (i = 1; i < 80; i++) {};
}

void writeBit(int b) {
 volatile int i;
 int delay1, delay2;
 if (b == 1) {
  delay1 = 1;
  delay2 = 80;
 } else {
  delay1 = 75;
  delay2 = 6;
 }
 P0.setDigitalValue(0);
 for (i = 1; i < delay1; i++) {};
 P0.setDigitalValue(1);
 for (i = 1; i < delay2; i++) {};
}
```

```
void sendskip() {
 writeBit(0);
 writeBit(0);
 writeBit(1);
 writeBit(1);
 writeBit(0);
 writeBit(0);
 writeBit(1);
 writeBit(1);
}

void writeByte(int byte) {
 int i;
 for (i = 0; i < 8; i++) {
  if (byte & 1) {
   writeBit(1);
  } else {
   writeBit(0);
  }
  byte = byte >> 1;
 }
}

int readBit() {
 volatile int i;
 P0.setDigitalValue(0);
 P0.setDigitalValue(1);
 for (i = 1; i < 20; i++) {};
 int b = P1.getDigitalValue();
 for (i = 1; i < 60; i++) {};
 return b;
}

int convert() {
 volatile int i;
 int j;
 writeByte(0x44);
 for (j = 1; j < 1000; j++) {
  for (i = 1; i < 900; i++) {};
  if (readBit() == 1)break;
 };
 return (j);
}

int readByte() {
 int byte = 0;
 int i;
 for (i = 0; i < 8; i++) {
  byte = byte | readBit() << i;
 };
 return byte;
}
```

The SPI bus can be something of a problem because it doesn't have a well defined standard that every device conforms to. Even so if you only want to work with one specific device it is usually easy to find a configuration that works - as long as you understand what the possibilities are.

The micro:bit has two SPI bus devices built into its processor a bus master and a bus slave. If you want to connect the micro:bit to SPI devices then it is the bus master that is of interest. If you want to use the micro:bit as a device connected to some other controller then you need to have it acting as a slave. This second scenario isn't as common and in this chapter we concentrate on using the micro:bit as a bus master.

## SPI Bus Basics

The SPI bus is very strange but commonly encountered as it is used to connect all sorts of devices from LCD displays, through real time clocks and AtoD converters. It is strange because there is no standard for it and different companies have implemented it in different ways. As a result you have to work harder to implement it in any particular case. However it usually works, which is a surprise for a bus with no standard or clear specification.

The reason it can be made to work is that you can specify a range of different operating modes, frequencies and polarities. This makes the bus slightly more complicated to use, but generally it is a matter of looking up how the device you are trying to work with implements the SPI bus and then getting the micro:bit to work in the same way.

The bus is odd in another way - it does not use bidirectional serial connections. There is a data line for the data to go from the master to the slave and a separate data line from the slave back to the master. That is, instead of a single data line that changes its transfer direction, there is one for data out and one for data in.

It is also worth knowing that the drive on the SPI bus is push-pull and not open collector/drain. This provides higher speed and more noise protection as the bus is driven in both directions. Also you don't need pullup resistors. There is a bidirectional mode where a single wire is used for the data, but the micro:bit doesn't support this.

The standard signal lines are

- MOSI Master Output Slave Input i.e. data to the slave
- MISO Master Input Slave Output i.e. data to the master
- SCLK Serial Clock which is always generated by the master

There can also be any number of SS - Slave Select - or CE Chip Select - lines which are usually set low to select which slave is being addressed.

Notice that unlike other buses, I2C for example, there are no SPI commands or addresses - only bytes of data. However slave devices do interpret some of the data as commands to do something or send some particular data.

The micro:bit has two SPI bus Masters, but only one is exposed on the GPIO connector. There are no standard CE lines, although it is easy and logical to assign Pin 16 to this task. This means that in principle you can only connect one SPI device to the micro:bit, although this restriction is easy to overcome by using additional GPIO lines.

The second SPI bus Master can be used just as easily as the first but you will have to allocate four GPIO lines to it and this is certain to mean loss of other functions.

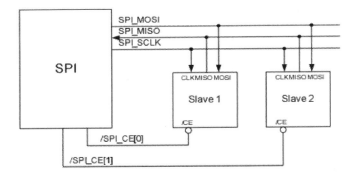

In principle the SPI bus master hardware can be connected to any four GPIO lines but the pins that are normally used are:

```
SPI Bus Pins
MICROBIT_PIN_P13   SCLK
MICROBIT_PIN_P14   MISO
MICROBIT_PIN_P15   MOSI
MICROBIT_PIN_P16   CE
```

Notice that the use of Pin 16 isn't a mandatory and it isn't part of the usual pin allocation lists or diagrams.

The data transfer on the SPI bus is also slightly odd. What happens is that the master pulls one of the chip selects low which activates a slave. Then the master toggles the clock SCLK and both the master and the slave send a single bit on their respective data lines. After eight clock pulses a byte has been transferred from the master to the slave and from the slave to the master. You can think of this as being implemented as a circular buffer .

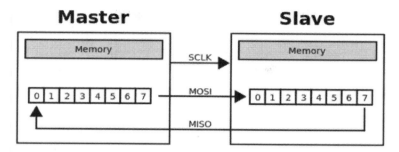

This full duplex data transfer is often hidden by the software and the protocol used. For example there is a single write function that also reads data from the slave - it readily should be called a read-write function.

The transfer is typically in groups of eight bits and usually most significant bit first but this isn't always the case. In general as long as the master supply clock pulses data is transferred.

Notice this circular buffer arrangement allows for slaves to be daisy chained with the output of one going to the input of the next. This makes the entire chain one big circular shift register. This makes it possible to have multiple devices with only a single chip select, but it also means any commands sent to the slaves are received by each one in turn. For example you could send a convert command to each AtoD converter in turn and receive back results from each one.

The final odd thing about the SPI bus is that there are four modes which define the relationship between the data timing and the clock pulse. The clock can be either active high or low - clock polarity CPOL and data can be sampled on the rising or falling edge of the clock - clock phase CPHA. All combinations of these two possibilities gives the four modes:

| SPI Mode* | Clock Polarity CPOL | Clock Edge CPHA | Characteristics |
|---|---|---|---|
| 0 | 0 | 0 | Clock active high data output on falling edge and sampled on rising |
| 1 | 0 | 1 | Clock active high data output on rising edge and sampled on falling |
| 2 | 1 | 0 | Clock active low data output on falling edge and sampled on rising |
| 3 | 1 | 1 | Clock active low data output on rising edge and sampled on falling |

*The way that the modes are named is common but not universal

There is often a problem trying to work out what mode a slave device uses. The clock polarity is usually easy and the Clock phase can sometimes be worked out from the data transfer timing diagrams bearing in mind:

- First clock transition in the middle of a data bit means CPHA=0
- First clock transition at the start of a data bit means CPHA=1

So to configure the SPI bus to work with a particular slave device you have to select the clock frequency, anything from 125kHz to 8MHz and set the clock mode to one of Mode0 thru Mode3.

Now we have to find out how to do all of this using the functions supplied.

## The SPI Functions

The most import thing to say is that to use the SPI bus you have to leave the framework and use the mbed SPI class. This isn't a big problem but the facilities that are provided are less extensive than you might be used to.

### Initialization

Before you can use the SPI bus you have to create an instance of the SPI class and specify the pins you are going to use. The constructor is:

```
SPI(PinName mosi, PinName miso, PinName sclk, PinName ssel=NC);
```

You can specify any of the pins as NC (not connected) and if you don't specify a CE line then it is not connected by default. A standard SPI object using the standard pins is:

```
SPI spi(MOSI, MISO, SCK);
```

If you need a CE line then use:

```
SPI spi(MOSI, MISO, SCK,  MICROBIT_ID_IO_P16);
```

Notice that all the constructor does is to set the CE pin up correctly. When you use the write function it doesn't automatically toggle the CE line - you have to do this job manually. As the initialization of the CE line by the constructor seems to interfere with the framework's initialization, your choices are to either control the CE line directly or not include it in the constructor and control it via the framework.

## Configuration

There are a two functions that set the format of operation.

The first sets the mode and the number of bits:

```
void format(int bits, int mode = 0);
```

where mode is set according to the table listed earlier and bits sets the number of bits between 4 and 16 to be transferred in a read/write operation.

The second simply sets the frequency of operation i.e. the clock frequency:

```
void frequency(int hz = 1000000);
```

The allowed frequencies are:

```
125 kbps
250 kbps
500 kbps
1 Mbps
2 Mbps
4 Mbps
8 Mbps
```

If you don't select one of these then the software selects the next highest.


## Data Transfer function

Because of the way the SPI bus uses a full duplex transfer you only need a single data transfer function, in this case called:

```
int write(int value);
```

This sends a block of data to the slave while receiving a single block sent back. The number of bits sent and received is set by the configuration to anything from 4 to 16. In practice this is a read/write function but you can always simply throw away the data from the slave or send meaningless data to the slave to create something that looks like a read/write pair.

It is important to realize the write function does not control any CE line you may have defined. You have to set the CE line high when the SPI bus is being initialized and then lower it just before you write data to the slave. You then return the CE line high after the data transfer is complete.

Now we come to a subtle point. What is the difference between transferring multiple bytes and repeated single bytes? The answer is that for each transfer the CE line has to be toggled. If you want to transfer ten bytes one byte at a time the you have to perform ten calls to write lowering the CE line before each call and raising it again before the next one. If you want to transfer ten bytes as a block then keep the CE line low until the tenth byte has been transferred. Sometimes this difference isn't important and you can transfer three bytes activating the CE line for each one or you can transfer three bytes keeping the CE line low until the transfer is over. However some slaves will abort the current multibyte operation if the chip select line is deactivated in the middle of a multibyte transfer.

It is important to realize that the nature of the transfer is that the first byte is sent at the same time that the first byte is received. That is, unlike other protocols, where you send some data and then get back some data. The whole transfer works a byte at a time, the first byte is sent while the first byte is being received, then the second byte is sent at the same time the second byte is being received and so on.

## A Loopback Example

Because of the way that data is transferred on the SPI bus, it is very easy to test that everything is working without having to add any components. All you have to do is connect MOSI to MISO so that anything sent to it is also received in a loopback mode.

First connect pin 14 to pin 15 using a jumper wire and start a new NetBeans project. As this is a loopback test we really don't need to configure the bus but for completeness:

```
spi.format(8,0);
spi.frequency(1000000);
```

Next we can send some data and receive it right back:

```
uint8_t read_data = spi.write(0xAA);
```

The hex value AA is useful in testing because it generates the bit sequence 10101010, which is easy to see on a logic analyzer. We can check that the received data matches the sent data in a variety of ways:

```
if( read_data== 0xAA) printf("data received correctly");
```

We can also create and use a CE line using GPIO pin 16:

```
MicroBitPin CS(MICROBIT_ID_IO_P16,
               MICROBIT_PIN_P16,
               PIN_CAPABILITY_DIGITAL );
```

To make the SPI bus work properly when connected to a real slave device, rather than just in loopback mode, we need to set the CE line high when we initialize the bus and then set it low before sending data.

Putting all of this together gives us the complete program:

```
#include "MicroBit.h"
SPI spi(MOSI, MISO, SCK);
MicroBitSerial serial(USBTX, USBRX);
MicroBitPin CS(MICROBIT_ID_IO_P16,
               MICROBIT_PIN_P16,
               PIN_CAPABILITY_DIGITAL);

int main() {
    CS.setDigitalValue(1);
    spi.format(8, 0);
    spi.frequency(1000000);
    CS.setDigitalValue(0);
    uint8_t read_data = spi.write(0xAA);
    CS.setDigitalValue(1);
    if (read_data == 0xAA) printf("data received correctly");
    release_fiber();
    return 0;
}
```

If you run the program and don't get the "data received correctly" message then the most likely reason is that you have connected the wrong two pins together or not connected them at all.

If you connect a logic analyzer to the four pins involved - 13,14, 15 and 16 you will see the data transfer:

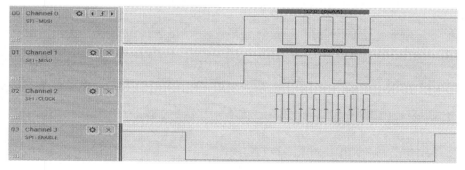

If you look carefully you will see the CS0 line go low before the master places the first data bit on the MOSI and hence on the MISO lines. Typically the CS line is held for at least three core clock cycles before transfer starts to allow the slave to get ready and held for at least one clock cycle when the transfer is complete. Notice that the clock rises in the middle of each data bit making this a mode 0 transfer. You can also see that the clock is measured to be 1MHz as promised.

If you want to transfer multiple bytes as a single operation then you can manually leave the CS low until all of the transfers are complete. However, you need to proceed depends on the slave device and you need to read the data sheet.

# Problems

The SPI bus is often a real headache because of the lack of a definitive standard, but in most cases you can make it work. The first problem is in discovering the characteristics of the slave device you want to work with. In general this is solved by a careful reading of the data sheet or perhaps by some trial and error, see the next chapter for an example.

If you are working with a single slave then generally things work once you have the SPI bus configuration set correctly. Where things are more difficult is if you have multiple devices on the same bus. Typically you will find SPI devices that don't switch off properly when they are not being addressed. In principle all SPI devices should present high impedance outputs (i.e. tristate buffers) when not being addressed, but some don't. If you encounter a problem you need to check that the selected slave is able to control the MISO line properly.

If you need more CS lines then you can allocate more GPIO lines to the job but these are in short supply. A better solution is to multiplex the GPIO lines to create additional chip selects. For example you can use standard GPIO lines as chip selects and connect four SPI slaves using a 2 to 4 decoder..

## Summary

- The SPI bus is often problematic because there is no SPI standard

- Unlike other serial buses it makes use of unidirectional connections.

- The data lines are MOSI master output slave input and MISO master input slave output.

- In addition there is a clock line - output from master and an unspecified number of select lines.

- Data is transferred from the master to the slave and from the slave to the master on each clock pulse in arranged as a circular buffer.

- The mbed library provides the basic function you need to work with the SPI bus and you can test the SPI bus using a simple loopback connection.

- Working with a single slave is usually fairly easy, working with multiple slaves can be more of a problem.

# Chapter 11
# AtoD With The SPI Bus

The SPI bus can be difficult to make work at first, but once you know how the slave works it gets easier. To demonstrate how it is done let's add eight channels of 12-bit AtoD using the MCP3008.

The micro:bit has a single analog to digital converter which can be connected to any of the GPIO lines designated as analog pins. Sometimes, however, this isn't enough. The MCP3000 family of AtoD convertors provides a simple, cheap and low cost solution. Although the MCP3008 with 8 AtoD inputs and the MCP3004 with 4 AtoD inputs at 10-bit precision are the best known, there are other devices in the family including 12- and 13-bit precision devices with differential inputs at around the same sort of cost $1 to $2.

In this chapter the MCP3008 is used because it is readily available and provides a good performance at low cost, but the other devices in the family work in the same way and could easily be substituted.

## The MCP3008

The MCP3008 is available in a number of different packages, but the standard 16-pin PDIP is the easiest to work with using a prototyping board. You can buy it from the usual sources including Amazon if you need one in a hurry. Its pinouts are fairly self explanatory:

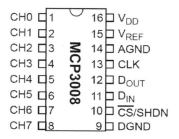

You can see that the analog inputs are on the left and the power and SPI bus connections are on the right. The conversion accuracy is claimed to be 10 bits, but how many of these bits correspond to reality and how many are noise depends on how you design the layout of the circuit.

You need to take great care if you need high accuracy. For example, you will notice that there are two voltage inputs VDD and VREF. VDD is the supply voltage that runs the chip and VREF is the reference voltage that is used to compare the input voltage.

Obviously if you want highest accuracy, VREF, which has to be lower than or equal to VDD, should be set by an accurate low noise voltage source. However in most applications VREF and VDD are simply connected together and the usual, low quality supply voltage is used as the reference. If this isn't good enough then you can use anything from a zener diode to a precision voltage reference chip such as the TL431. At the very least, however, you should add a 1uF capacitor between the VDD pin and the VREF pin to ground.

The MC3000 family implements a type of AtoD based on a technique called successive approximation. You don't need to know how it works to use the MC3000, but it isn't difficult. The idea is that first a voltage is generated equal to VREF/2 and the input voltage is compared to this. If it is less, the most significant bit is a zero; and if it is more or equal, then it is a one. At the next step the voltage generated is VREF/2 + VREF/4 and the comparison is repeated to generate the next bit.

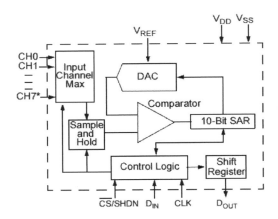

You can see that successive approximation fits in well with a serial bus as each bit can be obtained in the time needed to transmit the previous bit. However, the conversion is relatively slow and a sample and hold circuit has to be used to keep the input to the convertor stage fixed. The sample and hold takes the form of a 20pF capacitor and a switch. The only reason you need to know about this is that the conversion has to be complete in a time that is short compared to the discharge time of the capacitor. So for accuracy there is a minimum SPI clock rate as well as a maximum.

Also, to charge the capacitor quickly enough for it to follow a changing voltage, it needs to be connected to a low impedance source. In most cases this isn't a problem, but if it is you need to include an op amp.

If you are using an op amp buffer then you might as well implement an anti-aliasing filter to remove frequencies from the signal that are too fast for the AtoD to respond to. How all this works takes us into the realm of analog electronics and signal processing and well out of the scope of this book.

You can also use the AtoD channels in pairs - differential mode - to measure the voltage difference them. For example, in differential mode you measure the difference between CH0 and CH1, i.e. what you measure is CH1-CH0. In most cases you want to use all eight channels in single-ended mode. In principle you can take 200K samples per second, but only at the upper limit of the supply voltage (VDD=5V), falling to 75K samples per second at its lower limit (VDD=2.7V).

The SPI clock limits are a maximum of 3.6MHz at 5V and 1.35MHz at 2.7V. The clock can go slower, but because of the problem with the sample and hold mentioned earlier it shouldn't go below 10kHz.

How fast we can take samples is discussed later in this chapter.

## Connecting MCP3008 to micro:bit

The connection to the SPI bus is very simple and can be seen in the diagram below.

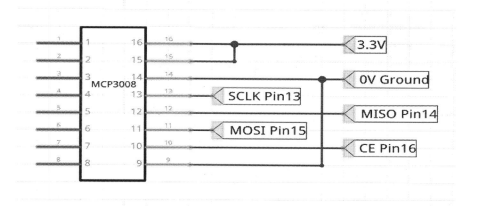

The only additional component that is recommended is a 1uF capacitor connected between pins 15 and 16 to ground mounted as close to the chip as possible. As discussed in the previous section, you might want a separate voltage reference for pin 15 rather than just using the 3.3V supply.

## Basic Configuration

Now we come to the configuration of the SPI bus. Taking into account the maximum clock frequencies for the device 3.6MHz at 5V and 1.35MHz at 2.7V and the need to maintain a minimum clock rate of 10KHz, using the default clock rate of 1MHz seems a reasonable starting point.

From the data sheet the CS has to be active low and the most significant bit first is the default for both the master and the slave. The only puzzle is what mode to use? This is listed in the data sheet if you look really carefully and it can be mode 0,0 with clock active high or mode 1,1 with clock active low. For simplicity we can use mode 0,0 which is mode0 in the mbed library. We now have enough information to initialize the slave:

```
spi.format(8, 0);
spi.frequency(1000000);
```

## The Protocol

Now we have the SPI initialized and ready to transfer data but what data do we transfer?

The SPI bus doesn't have any standard commands or addressing structure. Each device responds to data sent in different ways and sends data back in different ways. You simply have to read the data sheet to find out what the commands and responses are.

Reading the data sheet might be initially confusing because it says that what you have to do is send five bits to the slave - a START bit, a bit that selects its operating mode, and a 3-bit channel number. The operating mode is 1 for single ended and 0 for differential. Differential mode uses the channels in pairs to measure the voltage difference between them. In most cases you want to use single ended. So to read channel 3, i.e. 011, in single ended mode you would send the slave:

```
11011xxx
```

where xxx means don't care.

The response from the slave is that it holds its output in a high impedance state until the sixth clock pulse it then sends a 0 bit on the seventh followed by bit 9 of the data on clock eight.

That is the slave sends back:

```
x x x x x x 0 b9
```

where x means indeterminate and b9 is 0 or 1 according to the value of the ninth bit of the data. The remaining 9-bits are sent back in response to the next nine clock pulses, so you have to transfer three bytes to get all ten bits of data. This all makes reading the data in eight-bit chunks confusing.

The data sheet suggests a different way of doing the job that delivers the data more neatly packed into three bytes. What it suggests is to send a single byte:

```
00000001
```

The slave transfers random data at the same time which is ignored. The final 1 is treated as the start bit. If you now transfer a second byte with most significant bit indicating single or differential mode, then a three bit channel address and the remaining bits set to zero the slave will respond with the null and the top two bits of the conversion. Now all you have to do to get the final eight bits of data is to read a third byte:

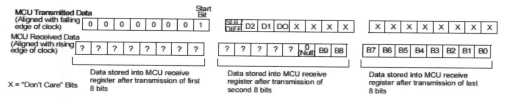

You can do it the first way that the data sheet describes, but this way you get two neat bytes containing the data with all the low order bits in their correct positions.

Using this information we can now write some instructions that read a given channel. For example, to read channel zero we first send a byte set to 0x01 as the START bit and ignore the byte the slave transfers. Next we send 0x80 to select single ended and channel zero and keep the byte the slave sends back as the high order two bits. Finally we send a zero byte so that we get the low order bits from the slave:

```
CS.setDigitalValue(0);
int buf[] = {0x01, 0x80, 0x00};
int readBuf[3];
int i;
for (i = 0; i < 3; i++) {
    readBuf[i] = spi.write(buf[i]);
}
CS.setDigitalValue(1);
```

Notice that the CS line is held low for the entire transaction.

To get the data out of readBuf we need to do some bit manipulation:

```
int data=((int)readBuf[1]&0x03)<< 8|(int)readBuf[2];
```

The first part of the expression extracts the low three bits from the first byte the slave sent and, as these are the most significant bits, they are shifted up eight places. The rest of the bits are then ORed with them to give the full 10-bit result. To convert to volts we use:

```
int volts=data*330/1023;
```

assuming that VREF is 3.3V.

Notice that we avoid floating point arithmetic by working with volts*100.

In a real application you would also need to convert the voltage to some other quantity like temperature or light level.

## Some Packaged Functions

This all works, but it would be good to have a function that read the AtoD on a specified channel. First let's write a function to transfer n bytes of data:

```
void transferBytes(int* buf,int*readBuf,int len){
  CS.setDigitalValue(0);
  int i;
  for (i = 0; i < len; i++) {
      readBuf[i] = spi.write(buf[i]);
  }
  CS.setDigitalValue(1);
}
```

Now we can write an AtoD function:

```
int readADC(uint8_t chan){
  int buf[] = {0x01,(0x08|chan)<<4,0x00};
  int readBuf[3];
  transferBytes(buf,readBuf,3);
  return (readBuf[1] & 0x03) << 8 |  readBuf[2];
}
```

Notice that this only works if the SPI bus has been initialized and set up correctly. An initialization function is something like:

```
void init_SPI(){
  CS.setDigitalValue(1);
  spi.format(8, 0);
  spi.frequency(1000000);
}
```

Now our main program can be just:

```
init_SPI();
int data=readADC(0x0);
int volts=data*330/1023;
printf("Voltage= %d.%d\n\r",volts/100,volts%100);
```

# How Fast

Once you have the basic facilities working the next question is always how fast does something work. In this case we need to know what sort of data rates we can achieve using this AtoD converter.

The simplest way of discovering this is to use the fastest read loop. For channel 5, say:

```
for(;;){
  int data=readADC(0x5);
}
```

With a 1MHz clock specified we do get a measured clock rate of 1MHz, but there are 29 microseconds between each reading. The sampling rate is measured to be 14kHz.

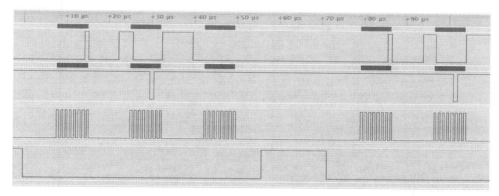

In principle, as it takes 24 clock periods to read the three bytes, the shortest time to read the data is 24 microseconds, but because of the delays it actually takes 71 microseconds. Some of this is due to the time to change the CS line. Clearly we could make this faster by using direct memory mapping.

Increasing the clock rate to 2MHz pushes the sampling rate to 36kHz, which is just fast enough to digitize audio as long as you don't waste too much time in the loop in processing. Changing the clock rate to 2Mhz,, pushes the sampling up to 18kHz which is just fast enough for most audio.

The fastest sampling rate achieved with the chips to hand was 21kHz with a clock rate of 4MHz. However the readings became increasingly unreliable in the low order bits.

Changing to direct memory mapping increased the sampling rate to 24kHz at a clock rate of 4Mhz. Unrolling the loop increased this to 26KHz but there was still an 8-microsecond pause between each byte which limits the speed of the transfer.

```
volatile unsigned int *outset =(unsigned int *)(0x50000000UL+0x508);
```

145

```
volatile unsigned int *outclr =(unsigned int *)(0x50000000UL+0x50C);
unsigned int mask = 1 << 16;

void transferBytes(int* buf,int*readBuf,int len){
    *outclr = mask;
    readBuf[0] = spi.write(buf[0]);
    readBuf[1] = spi.write(buf[1]);
    readBuf[2] = spi.write(buf[2]);
    *outset = mask;
}
```

The delay in reading the SPI bus comes down to the 8 microseconds between transferring each byte irrespective of the SPI clock frequency. The only way to do better than this is to directly access the SPI hardware. This is quite possible but we are approaching the maximum sampling rate of the device.

## Summary

Making SPI work with any particular device has four steps

1. Discover how to connect the device to the SPI put this is a matter of identifying pin outs and mostly what chip selects are supported.

2. Find out how to configure the SPI bus to work with the device. This is mostly a matter of clock speed and mode.

3. Identify the commands that you need to send to the device to get it to do something and what data it sends back as a response.

4. Find or workout what the relationship between the raw reading, the voltage and the quantity the voltage represents is.

# Chapter 12
# Serial Connections

The serial port is one of the oldest of ways of connecting devices together, but it is still very useful. The micro:bit has a single serial interface, but it can be directed to use any of the GPIO pins as Rx and Tx.

The software that powers the micro:bit does a lot to make the single tasking mbed environment that it is based on more like a multitasking operating system. The facilities it provides for working with the serial interface are extensive and it is important to know how it all works because it goes well beyond the raw serial facilities that it is based on.

## Serial Protocol

The serial protocol is very simple - it has to be because it was invented in the days when it was generated using electromechanical components, motors and the like. It was invented to make early teletype machines work and hence you will often find abbreviations such as TTY used in connection with it. As the electronic device used to work with serial is called a Universal Asynchronous Receiver/Transmitter the term UART is also often used.

The earliest standards are V24 and RS232. However, notice that early serial communications worked between $\pm24$V and later $\pm12$V. Today serial communications works at logic or TTL levels 0 to 5V or 0 to 3.3V. This voltage difference is a problem we will return to later. What matters is that, irrespective of the voltage, the protocol is always the same.

For the moment let's concentrate on the protocol, which as already mentioned is simple. The line rests high and represents a 0. When the device starts to transmit it first pulls the line low to generate a start bit. The width of this bit sets the transmission speed - all bits are the same width as the start bit. After the start bit there are a variable number, usually seven or eight, data bits, an optional single parity bit and finally one or two or zero stop bits.

Originally the purpose of the start bit was to allow the motors etc to get started and allow the receiving end to perform any timing corrections – the start bit determined the width of all subsequent bits. The stop bits were similarly there to give time for the motors to come back to their rest position. In the early days the protocol was used at very slow speeds - 300 baud, i.e. roughly 300 bits per second, was considered fast enough.

Today the protocol is much the same, but there is little need for multiple stop bits and communications is often so reliable that parity bits are dispensed with. Transmission speeds are also higher - typically 9600 or 115200 baud.

To specify what exact protocol is in use you will often encounter a short form notation – e.g. 9600 8 data bits no parity one stop bit would be written as 9600 8n1.

You can see the letter A 01111101 transmitted using 8n1 in the logic analyzer trace:

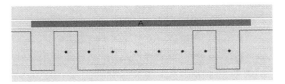

The first low is the start bit, then the eight dots show the ideal sampling positions for the receiver. The basic decoding algorithm for receiving serial data is to detect the start of the start bit and then sample the line at the center of each bit time. Notice that the final high on the right is the stop bit.

For a serial connection to work it is essential that the transmitter and the receiver are set to the same speed, data bits and parity. Serial interfaces most often fail because they are not working with the same settings.

A logic analyzer with a serial decoder option is an essential piece of equipment if you are going to anything complicated with serial interfacing.

What is a baud?

Baud rate refers to the basic bit time. That is, 300 baud has a start bit that is 1/300s wide. For 9600 a bit is 1/9600 wide, or roughly 104 microseconds. At 115200 baud a bit is 1/115200 or roughly 8.6 microseconds.

Notice baud rate doesn't equate to speed of sending data because there is an overhead in stop, start and perhaps parity bits to include in the calculation.

## Hardware

A simple serial interface has a transmit pin Tx and a receive pin Rx. That is, a full serial interface uses two wires for two-way communications.

Typically you connect the Tx pin on one device to the Rx pin on the other and vice versa. The only problem is that some manufacturers label the pins by what they should be connected to, not what they are, and you have to connect Rx to Rx and Tx to Tx which is not really helpful. You generally need to check with a scope, logic probe or meter which pin is which if you are in any doubt.

In addition to the Tx and Rx pins, a full serial interface also has a lot of control lines. Most of these were designed to help with old fashioned teleprinters and they are not often used. For example RTS (Request To Send) is a line that it used to ask permission to send data from the device at the other end of the connection, CTS (Clear To Send) is a line that indicates that it is okay to send data and so on. For most connections between modern devices you can ignore these additional lines and just send and receive data. If you need to interface to something that implements a complex serial interface you are going to have to look up the details and hand craft a program to interact with it. For the rest of this chapter we are going to work with Tx and Rx and ignore additional status and signaling lines.

The UART in the micro;bit's CPU can work independently of the rest of the hardware. That is, it will receive and transmit data while the CPU is getting on with other things. It can also be connected to any GPIO lines you care to use. Normally it is connected to pins that are part of the USB port. This means that, by default, sending and receiving serial data works over the USB port and if the PC it is connected to has a serial port driver you automatically have serial connection that works, assuming you have set the correct speed.

The fact that the serial device can be connected to any GPIO lines means that you can make use of it to talk to other devices directly and without the need to involve the USB port. You can even talk to a device connected to GPIO lines and echo what is going on to the USB serial port.

The micro:bit implements serial communications at 0 to 3.3V and connecting it to anything else will damage it. Note that PC-based serial ports usually use +13 to -13 and all RS232 compliant ports use a + to - voltage swing which is completely incompatible with the micro:bit and most other microprocessors. If you are using the default configuration with the serial device connected via the USB port this isn't a worry. However, if you want to use a GPIO line then you need to do something about level conversions.

To connect to the micro:bit you need a USB to TTL level serial interface that works between 0 and 3.3V. There are lots on the market. All you have to do is plug the USB port into the PC or device, install a driver and start to transmit data. If you want to work with the USB serial port then you will need a serial terminal on your desktop machine to connect to the micro:bit. For Windows users simply download PuTTY - search the internet for the website.

The default for the USB serial connection is 115200 baud 8 bits no parity and 1 stop bit. If you are using a PC and PuTTY you simply need to set PuTTY to 115200 and it should just work.

## Basic Serial Commands

There seem to be a lot of commands relating to the serial port. However, they fall into just three groups - initialization, writing and reading.

The initialization commands control how the port works. They all create or work with an instance of MicroBitSerial, but if you want to create an instance of your own don't create an instance of uBit. This simply causes a conflict with two instances of MicroBitSerial trying to control the hardware. If you want to use the other feature provide by uBit, the simplest thing to do is to create a global uBit and initialize it in the usual way. Then use its Serial property to access the MicroBitSerial object that has been created:

```
#include "MicroBit.h"
MicroBit uBit;
int main()
{
 uBit.init();
 uBit.serial.baud(115200);
 uBit.serial.send("A\r\n");
}
```

By default this connects to the USB serial so you should see an A printed on the serial console connected to the port.

If you want to create your own MicroBitSerial you can, but be careful not to create a uBit object and always create MicroBitSerial as a Global object.
To create the equivalent of the previous program you would use:

```
#include "MicroBit.h"
MicroBitSerial serial(USBTX, USBRX);
int main()
{
 serial.baud(115200);
 serial.send("A\r\n");
 release_fiber();
}
```

Notice that USBTX and USBRX give the GPIO pins to use to connect to the USB port.

For the rest of this chapter we will use the uBit serial property because this is by far the most common way of working. The constructor for the MicroBitSerial object takes the pins to be used as Tx and Rx as parameters:

```
MicroBitSerial( PinName tx, PinName  rx);
```

The default MicroBitSerial object created by the uBit object is set up using the constructor with USBTX and USBRX. There is also a version of the constructor that lets you set the buffer size:

```
MicroBitSerial( PinName tx,PinName rx,uint8_t rxBufferSize)
```

and also one to set the size of the Tx and Rx buffers separately:

```
MicroBitSerial( PinName tx,PinName rx,
                uint8_t  rxBufferSize,
                uint8_t  txBufferSize)
```

You can mostly ignore the buffer size, for the moment at least, and simply use the default buffer size.

Once you have a MicroBitSerial object you can set its baud rate using:

```
void baud( int baudrate)
```

This is currently the only setting you can change using the high level micro:bit framework. You can use a method inherited from deep down in the mbed framework:

```
void SerialBase::format(int bits, Parity parity, int stop_bits)
```

where mbed::RawSerial::Parity is one of

```
enum Parity {
    None = 0,
    Odd,
    Even,
    Forced1,
    Forced0
};
```

For example to set two stop bits you might use:

```
uBit.init();
uBit.serial.format(8,mbed::RawSerial::None,2);
uBit.serial.baud(115200);
uBit.serial.send("A\r\n");
```

The only problem with format is that there is no guarantee that it will not interact with the rest of the framework in some unexpected way - it doesn't seem to.

The final configuration function is very important if you want to communicate with anything other than a PC over the USB connection:

```
int redirect(PinName tx, PinName rx)
```

This changes the tx and rx pins to whatever you specify.

The rest of the configuration seems to transfer to the new pins as well. So, for example, to send something on physical Pin 1 on the edge connector (and receive on Pin 2) you would use:

```
uBit.init();
uBit.serial.format(8,mbed::RawSerial::None,2);
uBit.serial.baud(115200);
uBit.serial.redirect(MICROBIT_PIN_P1, MICROBIT_PIN_P2);
uBit.serial.send("A\r\n");
```

If you connect a logic analyzer to Pin 1 you will see the serial data for a letter A followed by a carriage return and line feed. Sending Data

We have already used the send function without really discussing it but sending data isn't the difficult part of using serial - receiving data is.

There are set of send functions which differ in what they allow you to send;

```
int sendChar(char c)
int send(ManagedString s)
int send(ManagedString s,MicroBitSerialMode mode)
int send(uint8_t *buffer,int bufferLen)
int send(uint8_t *buffer,int bufferLen,MicroBitSerialMode mode)
```

You can see that you can send a single char, a ManagedString or a buffer of bytes and this is usually more than enough to work with. In addition there is also a **putc** and **puts** which let you send a single character or an unmanaged string inherited from the mbed framework, but there seems to be little reason to use them.

You don't need putc because you have sendChar. You don't need puts because send will convert a standard C string into a managed string automatically. The only inherited method that seems useful is:

```
send_break()
```

which sends a low for longer than a character time. Some devices need a break signal to reset or do something special and this cannot be sent as a character code.

The mode parameter is slightly more important when you are receiving data, but it still has an effect when you send data.

There are three modes:

- ASYNC - the characters are sent to the buffer and the function returns at once.

- SYNC_SPINWAIT - the characters are sent to the buffer and your program (i.e. the calling fiber) will wait until they are all sent.

- SYNC_SLEEP - the characters are sent to the buffer and your program sleeps allowing other fibers to run.

The default is SYNC_SLEEP but notice that if you have a single fiber program there isn't a lot of difference between the two SYNCs. Notice that ASYNC allows your fiber to get on with things while the characters are being sent and this is often the most useful option.

## Reading Data

When programming a serial connection it is reading data that usually causes the most difficulty. Sending data is easy - you just send it, but receiving data requires you to know that there is some data to receive. In short, the problem is finding out when the other device has sent you something to process.

Basically there are only two ways of doing this. You can poll the receive buffer to detect when there is some data to read or you can set up an interrupt have it call a function when there is something to read. While the interrupt approach seems to have a lot going for it the simpler polling approach is often the better choice:

```
int read()
int read(MicroBitSerialMode mode)
ManagedString  read(int size)
ManagedString  read(int size,MicroBitSerialMode mode)
int read(uint8_t *buffer,int bufferLen)
int read(uint8_t *buffer,int bufferLen,MicroBitSerialMode mode)
```

The simple read command with or without mode specified reads a single character. These are often used in a loop to read characters until there are no more - but if you are going to do this you need to set the correct mode.

The ManageString function are fine as long as you know how many characters you are expecting. The read into a buffer has the same problem i.e. you need to specify the number of bytes to read.

As well as these standard functions there is also a pair of readUntil functions:

```
ManagedString readUntil(ManagedString delimiters)
ManagedString readUntil(ManagedString delimiters,
                        MicroBitSerialMode mode)
```

These will read the receive buffer until one of the delimiters included in the ManagedString are encountered. For example:

```
s=readUntil("\n");
```

will read characters from the receive buffer until it finds a new line code. Notice that the string matching is on per character basis so

```
s=readUntil("\n\r");
```

will stop on encountering a new line or a carriage return not a newline followed by a carriage return.

The modes work in the same way as for send but if you select ASYNC then the function return immediately if there is nothing in the receive buffer and they return a null of some sort.

- The read a character function returns MICROBIT_NO_DATA.
- The read ManagedString functions return as many characters as available or a null string if there are none.
- The readUntil will return a null if the delimiter isn't in the buffer.

The other modes hang your program until the request can be met. This is fine for sending data, but when you are receiving data you cannot be sure that the other device will ever send you anything to get you out of the spinwait or the sleep.

To see how this all might work let's write a simple polling loop that reads characters from the serial Rx and sends them to the serial Tx. If you use this with the terminal you will see characters echoed until you type an x.

```
uBit.init();
uBit.serial.baud(115200);
int c;
do {
    c=uBit.serial.read(ASYNC);
    if((char)c!=MICROBIT_NO_DATA)uBit.serial.send((char)c);
} while(c!='x');
```

This works but you might be thinking what a waste of processor power. This is true but you can put whatever processing you want to perform in the **do** loop and check the receive buffer only when the loop repeats.

You can use the same trick to send characters from the USBTX to another pin:

```
uBit.init();
uBit.serial.baud(115200);
int c;
do {
    c=uBit.serial.read(ASYNC);
    if(c!=MICROBIT_NO_DATA){
      uBit.serial.redirect(MICROBIT_PIN_P1, MICROBIT_PIN_P2);
      uBit.serial.send((char)c);
      uBit.serial.redirect(USBTX, USBRX);
    }
  } while((char)c!='x');
```

This works but there is a problem. Each time the redirect occurs a spurious character is transmitted, usually a poorly framed character that should be rejected by the other device as an error. This spurious character is a real problem because it stops you from writing a program that takes data from one serial port and sends it to another. If you have to rapidly switch between connections the spurious extra characters swamp the connection.

Notice that the read returns immediately in ASYNC mode. If you select any of the other modes then it only returns when there is a character received. In this case you don't need the if statement to test for a result. However, if the device you are connecting to never sends a character ,the loop hangs forever.

## Using Events

There is a tendency among IoT programmers to use interrupts too often. They are useful when you need to deal with a low priority event that occurs very rarely. For something that is important and very common you usually need to use a polling loop to keep up.

You still need to know how to use events to work with the serial port and there are some tricky things you have to get right.

There are two event sources that you can control:

```
int eventAfter(int len)
int eventAfter(int len,MicroBitSerialMode mode)
```

which trigger an event if there are len characters in the receive buffer and:

```
int eventOn(ManagedString delimeters)
int eventOn(ManagedString delimeters,MicroBitSerialMode mode)
```

which triggers an event if any of the specified delimeters are present in the receive buffer.

There are two things to notice when using these events. The first is that at the moment the framework does not allocate buffers until you have actually used the serial device. What this means is that you can set up a program that looks

155

reasonable but never fires a event because the receive buffer is never created. The second problem is that these events only fire once.

Both events have an ID of:

```
MICROBIT_ID_SERIAL
```

and respective values:

```
MICROBIT_SERIAL_EVT_HEAD_MATCH
MICROBIT_SERIAL_EVT_DELIM_MATCH
```

Notice that you can set the usual modes but SPINWAIT will return an error and SLEEP will pause the fiber and wait for the event.

As an example of using serial events let's write a program that simply copies characters to the LED display. The event handler is just:

```
void onChar(MicroBitEvent e) {
    ManagedString s = uBit.serial.read(1);
    uBit.serial.clearRxBuffer();
    uBit.display.scroll(s);
    uBit.serial.eventAfter(1);
};
```

The main program is:

```
int main() {
    uBit.init();
    uBit.serial.setRxBufferSize(20);
    uBit.serial.baud(115200);
    uBit.messageBus.listen(MICROBIT_ID_SERIAL,
        MICROBIT_SERIAL_EVT_HEAD_MATCH,
        onChar);
    uBit.serial.eventAfter(1);
    while (1)uBit.sleep(1000);
    release_fiber();
}
```

Notice that we have to do a setRxBufferSize call to make the framework actually create a buffer. The eventAfter function sets the event ready to happen and the while(1)sleep(1000) keep the fiber running.

Normally this is where the fiber would do something else while waiting for the event. Alternatively you could simply release the fiber and let the scheduler call the event handler.

The event handler is simple enough, but notice that we have to set eventAfter(1) to reset the event to happen a second time. These features of the framework might well change in future versions.

# Problems With Serial

The biggest problem with using micro:bit serial is that, even though you can connect it to different GPIO lines, there is only one serial hardware device, i.e. one UART. A standard problem when trying to multiplex it between different lines is that when the switch happens both the Rx and Tx buffers are swapped to the new pins.

For example, suppose you are connected to a device on pins 0 and 1 and you suddenly switch the UART to USBTX and USBRX. If there was data coming in on pin 1 then switching pins will cause all sorts of problems as it aborts the transfer and can crash the micro:bit.

In general, you have to make sure that all data traffic has stopped before you switch pins. You might think that this an easy task, but it can be very difficult because of the use of Async and Sleep modes, which can allow your fiber to do things while data is being received or transmitted.

# Chapter 13

# Getting On WiFi

The micro:bit has a radio that works in Bluetooth LE and point-to-point ad-hoc mode, but at the moment it lacks WiFi connectivity. The solution is to use the low cost ESP8266 to make the connection via the micro:bit's serial port. As we will make a lot of use of the micro:bit's serial port it is assumed that you know roughly how it works. In particular, it is assumed that you are familiar with the material in the previous chapter. Before we get on to the details of using the ESP8266 we need to find out what makes it special.

## The Amazing ESP8266

The ESP8266 is a very odd and amazing device. It is remarkably low cost, $5 or less, but it is a full microprocessor with GPIO lines, RAM and built in WiFi. It is built by a Chinese company Espressif Systems but there are a number of copies on the market. The proliferation of devices and software revisions makes it difficult to work with, but it is well worth the effort.

While you can set up a development system yourself and program the ESP8266 to do almost anything, it comes with built-in software that allows it to be used as a WiFi module for other processors. This is how we are going to use it to give the micro:bit a WiFi capability.

The ESP8266 connects to the micro:bit using the serial port. The micro:bit controls it and transfers data using a system of AT commands. These were commonly used to control modems and other communication equipment and they still are used in mobile phone modems.

The module used in this chapter is the ESP-01 which is widely available from many different sources but they all look like the photo:

There is another version, the ESP-07, which comes with a screen RF stage and other advantages and this should also work.

A bigger problem is that there are new versions of the firmware and some of these might not work in exactly the same way. However, it should be easy to make the changes necessary.

## Connecting the ESP8266 ESP-01

There a number of minor problems in using the ESP8266. The first is that it comes with an 8-pin male connector which is not prototype board friendly. The best solution to this is to use some jumper cables - female to male - to connect it to the prototype board, or use female-to-female cables to connect directly to the micro:bit breakout board. A second problem is caused by the fact that the device is powered from a 3.3V supply. This might tempt you to try to power it from the micro:bit's 3.3V supply.

**This will not work.**

The ESP8266 takes a lot of current, 300mA or so, when transmitting. The micro:bit cannot supply this much current. You need to use a separate 3.3V power supply. Of course you can use this to power both the ESP8266 and the micro:bit and in some situations this would be an advantage. You can use one of the many low cost prototyping board power supplies with no problems:

The pin out of the ESP-01 is usually shown from the component side, but in fact the pins that you want to connect to are on the other side. To make things easier the two views are given in the diagram:

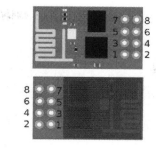

The pin functions are:

    1 Ground   connect to ground
    2 TXO      the serial tx pin
    3 GPIO2    ignore
    4 CHPD    chip enable connect to 3.3V
    5 GPIO0    ignore
    6 RST       reset leave unconnected
    7 RXI       the serial rx pin
    8 VDD     supply voltage connect to 3.3V

From the pinouts you should be able to work out the way the ESP8266 has to be connected to the micro:bit. If we use P0 as Tx from the micro:bit and P1 as Rx to the micro:bit we have to connect ESP-01 pin 7 to P0, pin 2 to P1 and ESP-01 pins 8 and 4 to the external power supply. To make it all work we also have to connect ESP-01 pin 1 to the ground of the external power supply ground and to the ground of the micro:bit, as shown:

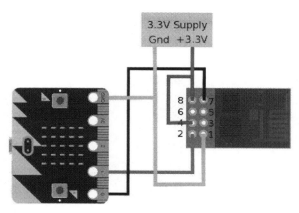

## AT Commands

The key idea in using the ESP8266 is that the micro:bit has to send an AT command, literally the characters AT, followed by other command strings. The command has to end with \r\n for the ESP8266 to take notice of it.

You can find a fill list of commands at the Espressif website, but the most important are:

| | |
|---|---|
| AT | Attention |
| AT+RST | Reset the board |
| AT+GMR | Firmware version |
| AT+CWMODE= | Operating Mode |
| | 1. Client 2. Access Point 3. Client and Access Point |
| AT+CWJAP= | Join network |
| AT+CWLAP | View available networks |
| AT+CWQAP | Disconnect from network |
| AT+CIPSTATUS | Show current status as socket client or server |
| AT+CIPSTART= | Connect to socket server |
| AT+CIPCLOSE | Close socket connection |
| AT+CIFSR | Show assigned IP address when connected to network |
| AT+CIPMUX= | Set connection |
| | 0. Single Connection 1. Multi-Channel Connection |
| AT+CIPSERVER= | Open the Socket Server |
| AT+CIPMODE= | Set transparent mode |
| AT+CIPSTO= | Set auto socket client disconnect timeout from 1-28800s |
| +IPD | Data |

This is just a very general overview and omits the commands that allow the device to work as an access point. It is assumed that client mode is the more common application, but it isn't difficult to extend this example to access point operation.

### Setup

We need a function to set up the hardware ready to communicate with the device:

```
void initWiFi() {
    uBit.serial.redirect(Tx, Rx);
    uBit.serial.baud(115200);
    uBit.serial.setRxBufferSize(500);
}
```

The pins that we are using are P0 and P1, but to allow for other choices Tx and Rx are defined as constants at the start of the program:

```
#define Tx MICROBIT_PIN_P0
#define Rx MICROBIT_PIN_P1
```

The model of ESP8266 used worked at 115200 baud by default. Newer models and up-dated firmware is reported to work at 9600 baud. If this is the case you need to modify the data rate and/or change the ESP8266's baud rate.

## Attention!

To start with the easiest, but possibly least useful, command let's implement some functions that test that we have a connection to the device - always a good thing to start with.

In this section we develop the first of a number of functions that send a command to the device and get back a response. To do this we need a few other functions to help and these are reused in other AT functions. Once you have one AT function the rest are very similar so it is worth spending some time following how this most simple AT function works.

If you send the string AT\r\n then the ESP8266 replies with a single "OK". This proves that the serial interface is working and there isn't much point in moving on until you have tested that AT works.

The AT function is simply:

```
int ATWiFi() {
    uBit.serial.send("AT\r\n", SYNC_SPINWAIT);
    return 1;
}
```

You have to use SPINWAIT because things go wrong when you let the fiber continue to process while the data is being transmitted.

This is the most basic form of function that will do the job, but it isn't really practical. We need to check that it works and we need to get some feedback. We could read what is sent back and then display it on the LED display. This would work, but reading the LED display is very slow. A better idea is to send the data to the USB serial console when in a "debug" mode.

The problem with this is that every time you switch pins the serial device generates spurious characters. If we switch after receiving the entire message rather than on each character we can minimize the spurious characters - which the ESP8266 seems to ignore. A function to swap to and from the USB pins and send the data is easy:

```
void debug(ManagedString s) {
    uBit.serial.redirect(USBTX, USBRX);
    uBit.serial.send(s, SYNC_SPINWAIT);
    uBit.serial.redirect(Tx, Rx);
}
```

Now all we need to do is read the data sent back from the device. The simplest way of doing this is to wait for a period of time that means that the device has to have sent the data or there is something wrong. As 115200 baud allows for more than 100 characters in 10 milliseconds and 9600 baud takes just more than 100 milliseconds, you can estimate the time you need to wait for any packet of text to be delivered. As the response to the AT request only sends a few characters waiting 150 milliseconds is more than enough at any baud rate. We can then read the entire buffer:

```
uBit.sleep(150);
ManagedString s = uBit.serial.read(500, ASYNC);
```

Reading in ASYNC mode means that the function will return as many characters are in the buffer as a managed string.

If the AT command has been successful it returns a string containing "OK". One of the problems of working with AT commands is that they don't have an exact syntax and there is no formal "end of message" signal.

By observation, any successful command does end with "OK" and if you can't find "OK" in the response then you either haven't read it all or there has been an error. Clearly we need a way to test if a string contains "OK";

```
int find(ManagedString c, ManagedString s) {
    int i;
    for (i = 0; i < (s.length() - c.length()); i++) {
        if (c == s.substring(i, c.length())) break;
    }
    if (i == (s.length() - c.length())) return 0;
    return 1;
}
```

This is the simplest string scanning function that will do the job. It only checks that the string c is in s once and it will find c if it is embedded in another word. So it will find "OK" in "NotOK" for example.

With all of this we can now finish the ATWiFi function:

```
int ATWiFi() {
    uBit.serial.send("AT\r\n", SYNC_SPINWAIT);
    uBit.sleep(150);
    ManagedString s = uBit.serial.read(500, ASYNC);
    if (DEBUG)debug("\n\rAT \n\r" + s + "\n\r");
    return find("OK", s);
}
```

If the constant DEBUG is a 1 then the string is printed to the USB port and you can examine it:

```
#define DEBUG 1
```

## Program Listing

Putting all this together with a main program:

```
#include "MicroBit.h"

MicroBit uBit;

void initWiFi();
int ATWiFi();
int find(ManagedString c, ManagedString s);
void debug(ManagedString s);

#define Tx MICROBIT_PIN_P0
#define Rx MICROBIT_PIN_P1

#define DEBUG 1

int main() {
    initWiFi();
    ATWiFi();
    while (1)uBit.sleep(1000);
    release_fiber();
}
void initWiFi() {
    uBit.serial.redirect(Tx, Rx);
    uBit.serial.baud(115200);
    uBit.serial.setRxBufferSize(500);
}

int ATWiFi() {
    uBit.serial.send("AT\r\n", SYNC_SPINWAIT);
    uBit.sleep(150);
    ManagedString s = uBit.serial.read(500, ASYNC);
    if (DEBUG)debug("\n\rAT \n\r" + s + "\n\r");
    return find("OK", s);
}

void debug(ManagedString s) {
    uBit.serial.redirect(USBTX, USBRX);
    uBit.serial.send(s, SYNC_SPINWAIT);
    uBit.serial.redirect(Tx, Rx);
}
```

```
int find(ManagedString c, ManagedString s) {
    int i;

    for (i = 0; i < (s.length() - c.length()); i++) {
        if (c == s.substring(i, c.length())) break;
    }

    if (i == (s.length() - c.length())) return 0;
    return 1;
}
```

When you run this program then you should see:

```
AT
OK
```

printed on the serial console.

If you don't there are five possible reasons:

1.  You have connected the wrong pins - check
2.  The power supply you are using is inadequate - check/replace
3.  The serial console isn't working - check you can see any message
4.  The baud rate is wrong - try 9600
5.  The ESP8266 is broken - try another

## Some Utility Functions

Before we get into the details of connecting to a network and transferring data it is worth constructing some useful utility functions.

The need to wait for an "OK" or similar response is so common that it is worth having a function to do the job:

```
int  waitForWiFi(ManagedString target,int retry,int pause){
    ManagedString s;
        do {
            uBit.sleep(pause);
            if(s.length()>500)s="";
            s = s + uBit.serial.read(500, ASYNC);
            retry--;
        } while (find(target, s) == 0 && retry != 0);
        if (DEBUG)debug("\n\r" + s + "\n\r");
        return retry;
    }
```

Notice that now we can specify the target, a pause in milliseconds between polling attempts, and a timeout in terms of how many retries before the function gives up. Notice that the function returns 0 if there was a failure and the retry loop timed out and the number of retries remaining otherwise.

Using this utility function the ATWiFi function can be written:

```
int ATWiFi() {
    uBit.serial.send("AT\r\n", SYNC_SPINWAIT);
    return waitForWiFi("OK",150,10);
}
```

This is a lot shorter and easier to understand.

Assuming that you have managed to make the AT command work, it is time to move on to other AT commands. The first useful command is to find the Version number of the firmware. This is more or less the same as the AT function, but the command is AT+GMR and we get back more data - hence the longer wait time:

```
int getVersionWiFi() {
    uBit.serial.send("AT+GMR\r\n", SYNC_SPINWAIT);
    return waitForWiFi("OK",200,10);
}
```

The device in use returned:

```
AT+GMR
AT version:0.60.0.0(Jan 29 2016 15:10:17)
SDK version:1.5.2(7eee54f4)
Ai-Thinker Technology Co. Ltd.
May  5 2016 17:30:30
OK
```

The manual says that it should return AT, SDK and the time it was compiled, so we get a little extra with this third party device.

Another useful function is Reset. The device often gets stuck and then a reset is all that you can try. This is a software reset; another option is to use a GPIO line to connect to reset pin 6. By controlling this line you can force the device to hard reset. The soft reset command is AT+RST and all you get back in theory is "OK", but in practice the device sends a few hundred bytes of configuration data:

```
int resetWiFi() {
    uBit.serial.send("AT+RST\r\n", SYNC_SPINWAIT);
    return waitForWiFi("OK", 1000, 10);
}
```

The final utility function is to set the serial connection parameters to 115200, 8 bits, 1 stop bit, no parity, no flow control:

```
int setUARTWiFi() {
 uBit.serial.send("AT+UART_CUR=115200,8,1,0,0\r\n",SYNC_SPINWAIT);
 return waitForWiFi("OK", 200, 10);
}
```

If you change the baud rate to something other than what is in use you will, of course, lose communication with the device until you reconfigure the micro:bit's serial connection.

## Configuring WiFi

The first thing we need to configure is the operating mode. The ESP8622 can operate as an access point, i.e. it can allow other devices to connect to it. However, in most cases you will want it to work in client mode, connecting to your existing WiFi.

### Mode

A function to set its operating mode is:

```
int modeWiFi(int mode) {
  ManagedString cmd="AT+CWMODE_CUR="+ManagedString(mode)+"\r\n";
  uBit.serial.send(cmd, SYNC_SPINWAIT);
  return waitForWiFi("OK", 200, 10);
}
```

Notice that now we are constructing the command to send to the device in a separate step. If you try and do this on the fly in the function call, the rate of transmission of the serial data varies and the device can time out. In practice, construct all commands to send to the device first and then send them.

In this case the command is:

```
AT+CWMODE_CUR=n
```

where n is 1 for client, 2 for access point and 3 for both. If you want to make the change permanent then change CUR to DEF and the setting is stored in Flash. Older devices do not support CWMODE_CUR. Simply change it to CWMODE, which is deprecated.

To set client you would call:

```
modeWiFi(1);
```

and see OK sent back.

### Scan

The scan function is one that everyone wants to try out, but in practice it isn't very useful. Why would you want a list of WiFi networks? There are some applications for this function, but not as many as you might think. In most cases you simply want to connect to a known WiFi network , which is what we do in the next section.

The scan command is easy - just send AT+CWLAP and the device sends you a complete list of WiFi networks. The problem is that scanning takes a long time and often hangs. This is one case where we really need to specify a long timeout:

```
int scanWiFi() {
    uBit.serial.send("AT+CWLAP\r\n", SYNC_SPINWAIT);
    return waitForWiFi("OK", 500, 50);
}
```

Sometimes the loop completes with a full list, sometimes it doesn't. It depends on the WiFi networks that are available and how they reply to requests.

## Connecting to WiFi

Our final and most useful functions connect the device to a known WiFi network. All you have to do is supply the SSID and password. There are other versions of the command that allow you to specify the connection more precisely, but this general form is the most useful.

Connection to a network takes a while and there is quite a lot of data sent back, so we need to use the retry count loop introduced in the scan function:

```
int connectWiFi(ManagedString ssid, ManagedString pass) {
 ManagedString cmd="AT+CWJAP_CUR=\""+ssid+"\",\""+pass+"\"\r\n";
 uBit.serial.send(cmd, SYNC_SPINWAIT);
 return waitForWiFi("OK", 200, 20);
}
```

If you have an older device you might need to change CWJAP_CUR to the deprecated CWJAP command.

There is also a CWJAP_DEF command that will save the connection in the Flash memory.

The connection is made using:

```
connectWiFi("myWiFi","myPassword");
```

After a few seconds you should see:

```
AT+CWJAP_CUR="myWiFi","myPassword"
WIFI DISCONNECT
WIFI CONNECTED
WIFI GOT IP

OK
```

Once you are connected and the "WIFI GOT IP" message has been received you can ask what the IP address is:

```
int getIPWiFi() {
    uBit.serial.send("AT+CIFSR\r\n", SYNC_SPINWAIT);
    return waitForWiFi("OK", 200, 10);
}
```

Of course, if you really need to know the IP address within a program you need to extract it from the string. The device replies with:

```
IP address:
AT+CIFSR
+CIFSR:STAIP,"192.168.253.4"
+CIFSR:STAMAC,"5c:cf:7f:16:97:ab"

OK
```

which makes it very easy to get the IP address even without the help of a regular expression.

## Getting a Web Page

Now that we have so many functions we can tackle the two standard tasks in using the TCP stack - getting and sending data as a client and as a server.

First we tackle the problem of acting as a client. This isn't as common a requirement as you might expect because most of the time devices like the micro:bit are used to supply data to other servers, not the other way round. However, it is worth seeing how it is done.

It doesn't matter if you are implementing a client or a server you make use of sockets which represent the basic TCP connection. What you do with this connection is up to you. For example, if you send HTTP headers on an appropriate port then you can fetch or deliver a web page, i.e. HTTP over TCP. However, what data you actually send and receive over a socket connection is up to you and/or the protocol you are trying to use.

Hence the first thing we have to do is set up a socket connection between the client, i.e. the micro:bit, and the server.

```
int getWebPageWiFi(ManagedString URL,ManagedString page) {
  ManagedString cmd = "AT+CIPSTART=\"TCP\",\"" + URL + "\",80\r\n";
  uBit.serial.send(cmd, SYNC_SPINWAIT);
  if (waitForWiFi("OK", 100, 20) == 0) return 0;
```

You pass the URL to the function as an IP address or as a full URL, but the device looks up domain names using a fixed set of DNS servers.

It is recommended that you use an IP address especially when testing. The CIPSTART command opens a socket to the specified IP address and port. You can also specify a TCP or UDP connection:

```
AT+CIPSTART=type, IP, port
```

In this case we open port 80 on the specified IP address. If it works you will get back a message something like:

```
Connect
AT+CIPSTART="TCP","192.168.253.23",80
CONNECT

OK
```

Now we have a socket open we can send some data to the server and wait for some data to be sent back to us. This is the most difficult part of using the micro:bit on the web. If you request a web page then it is fairly likely that the data you get back is going to be too much to hold in memory. You either have to load a very small web page - a few hundred bytes - or process it on the fly as the data comes in. For this example the web page is served by a small sensor that returns a JSON temperature and humidity reading. The sensor is another micro:bit and the web server is described in the next section.

To send data over a socket you use CIPSEND, which will send any data you specify to the server. As already made clear, what you send is a matter for whatever protocol you are using over the socket. In this case it is HTTP and we are going to send headers corresponding to a GET request for index.html

```
ManagedString http = "GET /index.html
HTTP/1.0\r\nHost:192.168.253.23\r\n\r\n";
```

There are two headers:

```
GET /index.html HTTP/1.0
Host:192.168.253.23
```

Note that an HTTP request always ends with two blank lines.

To send this request we use the CIPSEND command which specifies the number of characters that are to follow:

```
cmd = "AT+CIPSEND=" + ManagedString(http.length()) + "\r\n";
uBit.serial.send(cmd, SYNC_SPINWAIT);
```

Now we have to send the number of bytes/ characters that we specified in the CIPSEND but first we wait for a ">" to indicate that the device is ready to receive the data:

```
s = "";
retry = 40;
do {
    uBit.sleep(100);
    s = s + uBit.serial.read(500, ASYNC);
    retry--;
} while (find(">", s) == 0 && retry != 0);
uBit.serial.send(http, SYNC_SPINWAIT);
```

What happens next depends on the server. As a result of the HTTP GET the server will now send data over the WiFi link and the device will send this over the serial connection as soon as it gets it. Notice we can't use the waitFor function because it might swap the serial lines and cause a spurious character to be transmitted.

Notice that this data is not a direct response to a command and so the device prefixes it with:

```
+IPD,len:
```

The +IPD makes it clear to the client that is a packet of data sent from the server. The len value gives the number of characters sent after the colon.

In principle what your program should do next is sit in a polling loop looking for +IPD. It should then read the digits between the comma and the colon and convert this to an integer. Finally it should then read exactly that number of characters from the serial port.

This can be done, but for a demonstration we simply read any data that is presented on the serial port for a reasonable amount of time in an attempt to capture all of the data. Notice that this is a fine balance between avoiding a buffer overrun because you don't read it often enough and not waiting long enough for all of the data.

There is also the problem that you can run out of memory, about 700 bytes seems to be the limit for the program as presented:

```
retry = 100;
do {
    uBit.sleep(100);
    s = s + uBit.serial.read(500, ASYNC);
    retry--;
} while (s.length() < 500 && retry != 0);

    if (DEBUG)debug("\n\rPage\n\r" + s + "\n\r");
    return 1;
}
```

The test website sends a very small amount of data and the result is:

```
+IPD,17:HTTP/1.0 200 OK

+IPD,99:Server: BaseHTTP/0.6 Python/3.2.3
Date: Thu, 14 Jul 2016 16:42:37 GMT
Content-type: text/html

+IPD,127:<html><head><title>Temperature</title></head><body><p>Tempe
rature:31.43</br>{"humidity":0,"airtemperature":0}</p></body></html>
CLOSED
```

You can see that there are three "packets" of data - 17 characters, 99 characters and finally 127 characters. In principle you could process the +IPD characters as they come in and work out how many characters to read. However, you still wouldn't know how many packets to expect.

Reading data from the web or any other protocol is limited to only small amounts of data - the example above is typical.

## A Web Server

The most common use for an internet connection on a small device like the micro:bit is to allow another device to request data. It is fairly easy to create a web server running on the ESP8266, but don't expect Apache or anything advanced. All you can reasonably do is accept a connection and send a web page or two back to the client.

The key differences between client and server mode is that in server mode the device constantly "listening" for clients to make TCP connections on the port. When the device receives a connection it reads all of the data the client sends and passes it on via the serial port to the the micro:bit. This means that in server mode the micro:bit has to be constantly on the lookout for new data from the ESP8266. You can do this using an interrupt, but for simplicity this example uses a polling loop.

There is another difference between client mode and server mode - there can be multiple TCP connections from as many clients that try to connect. The solution to this problem is that the ESP8226 assigns each TCP socket connection an id number and this is what you need to use to make sure you send the data to the right place.

Let's see how it all works.

Assuming we are already connected to WiFi and have an IP address, we can set up a server quite easily. First we need to use the CIPMUX =1 to set the device into multiple connection mode. You cannot start a server if CIPMUX=0, the default single connection mode.  Once multiple connections are allowed you can create server using CIPSERVER=1,port.

In this example we are using port 80 the standard HTTP port but you can change this to anything you want.

```
int startServerWiFi() {
    uBit.serial.send("AT+CIPMUX=1\r\n", SYNC_SPINWAIT);
    if (waitForWiFi("OK", 100, 20) == 0) return 0;

    uBit.serial.send("AT+CIPSERVER=1,80\r\n", SYNC_SPINWAIT);
    if (waitForWiFi("OK", 100, 20) == 0) return 0;
```

If you run just this part of the program you will see the response:

```
AT+CIPMUX=1

OK

AT+CIPSERVER=1,80
no change

OK
```

Now we just have to wait for a client to make a connection and send some data. This is done simply by reading the serial input and checking for "+IPD":

```
for (;;) {
    s="";
    do {
        uBit.sleep(100);
        if(s>500)s="";
        s = uBit.serial.read(500, ASYNC);
    } while (find("+IPD", s) == 0);
    if (DEBUG)debug("\n\rClient Connected\n\r" + s + "\n\r");
```

Notice the start of the outer infinite loop. What we are going to do is check for a connection, service the connection with some data and then go back to checking for another connection - hence the outer infinite loop, the server loop.

Once we have a connection it will be formatted so that the id is just after the "+IPD". In multiconnection mode the received data has the format:

```
+IPD,id, rest of data
```

We now need to extract the id so we can use it to communicate with the client. This is just some standard string handling, but it is still messy:

```
int b = find("+IPD", s);
s = s.substring(b + 1, s.length());
b = find(",", s);
s = s.substring(b + 1, s.length());
b = find(",", s);
ManagedString id = s.substring(0, b );
if (DEBUG)debug("\n\rTCP id:" + id + "\n\r");
```

The algorithm is:

- Find "+IPD" and trim the string so that it is the start.
- Find the first comma and trim the string so that it is the start.
- Find the next comma and extract the characters from the start of the string to the next comma.

Now we have the id we can communicate with the client, but first we need something to send. As with all HTTP transactions, we have to send some headers and then some data. There are a lot of possible headers you could send, but a reasonable minimum that works with most browsers is:

```
ManagedString headers = "HTTP/1.0 200 OK\r\n";
headers = headers + "Server: micro:bit\r\n";
headers = headers + "Content-type: text/html\r\n\r\n";
```

You can include time stamps and lots of other useful information, but this is simple and it works. Notice the blank line at the end of the headers - this is vital. The browser will ignore everything sent to it if you don't have a blank line at the end of the headers.

The html data is a simple JSON-style data object giving humidity and temperature:

```
ManagedString html ="<html><head><title>Temperature</title></head>
 <body>{\"humidity\":81%,\"airtemperature\":23.5C}</p></body>
 </html>\r\n";
ManagedString data=headers+html;
```

Of course, in a real sensor you would add live data into the HTML in place of the 81% and 23.5%. Notice that it is easier to combine the headers and the data into a single data string. The only reason for defining them as two separate strings is to make it easier to see what they contain.

Now we want to send the data to the client. This is just a matter of using the CIPSEND command again, this time with id specified as the first parameter:

```
CIPSEND=id,data length
```

and we wait for the response ">" before sending the data.

Notice that we don't have to open a TCP socket as we did in the case of acting as a client. The TCP socket has already been opened by the client connecting to the server and when the transaction is complete we can close it.

```
ManagedString cmd = "AT+CIPSEND="+id +","+
ManagedString(data.length()) + "\r\n";
uBit.serial.send(cmd, SYNC_SPINWAIT);
s = "";
int retry = 40;
do {
    uBit.sleep(100);
    s = s + uBit.serial.read(500, ASYNC);
    retry--;
  } while (find(">", s) == 0 && retry != 0);
```

Now, at last, we can send the data to the client:

```
uBit.serial.send(data, SYNC_SPINWAIT);
if (waitForWiFi("OK", 100, 100) == 0) return 0;
if (DEBUG)debug("\n\rData Sent\n\r");
```

and wait for it to complete.

Finally we close the connection and complete the loop to wait for another connection:

```
    cmd = "AT+CIPCLOSE=" + id + "\r\n";
    uBit.serial.send(cmd, SYNC_SPINWAIT);
    if (waitForWiFi("OK", 100, 100) == 0) return 0;
  };
}
```

Try it out with a main program something like:

```
int main() {
    uBit.init();
    initWiFi();
    modeWiFi(1);
    connectWiFi("ssid","pass");
    getIPWiFi();
    startServerWiFi();
}
```

You should now be able to connect to the IP address that is displayed and retrieve the web page that displays:

```
{"humidity":81%,"airtemperature":23.5C}
```

## Where Next?

There are a lot of WiFi commands that haven't been covered in this chapter, but now that you have seen examples of most of the basic types and encountered the typical problems that occur you should be able to implement any that you need.

The biggest problem in working with the micro:bit in serial mode it the limited amount of memory. If your program seems to have a tendency to simply "go quiet" on you then suspect that you are creating a ManagedString that is just too large. This is not a big problem when it comes to acting as a server, but it is for a client trying to process a lot of data.

There may also be better ways to handle the serial interaction between the two devices, but the method presented does seem to work reasonably well. If thing get in a mess then the retry limits usually reset the entire transaction if you wait long enough.

There is still going to be the occasional unexplained crash and in this case the best solution is to use the soft reset command. It is also worth mentioning that the server program as presented does not actually handle multiple connections. It has to finish dealing with one connection before it can deal with a second.

## Complete Listing

```
#include "MicroBit.h"

MicroBit uBit;
void initWiFi();
int ATWiFi();
int resetWiFi();
int setUARTWiFi();
int scanWiFi();
int getIPWiFi();
int modeWiFi(int mode);
int connectWiFi(ManagedString ssid, ManagedString pass);
int getWebPageWiFi(ManagedString URL, ManagedString page);
int getVersionWiFi();
int startServerWiFi();

int waitForWiFi(ManagedString target, int retry, int pause);
int find(ManagedString c, ManagedString s);
void debug(ManagedString s);

#define Tx MICROBIT_PIN_P0
#define Rx MICROBIT_PIN_P1

#define DEBUG 1

int main() {
    uBit.init();
    initWiFi();
    modeWiFi(1);
    connectWiFi("ssid", "password");
    getIPWiFi();
    startServerWiFi();
    release_fiber();
}

void initWiFi() {
    uBit.serial.redirect(Tx, Rx);
    uBit.serial.baud(115200);
    uBit.serial.setRxBufferSize(500);
}

int ATWiFi() {
    uBit.serial.send("AT\r\n", SYNC_SPINWAIT);
    return waitForWiFi("OK", 150, 10);
}
```

```
int getVersionWiFi() {
    uBit.serial.send("AT+GMR\r\n", SYNC_SPINWAIT);
    return waitForWiFi("OK", 200, 10);
}

int resetWiFi() {
    uBit.serial.send("AT+RST\r\n", SYNC_SPINWAIT);
    return waitForWiFi("OK", 1000, 10);
}

int setUARTWiFi() {
  uBit.serial.send("AT+UART_CUR=115200,8,1,0,0\r\n", SYNC_SPINWAIT);
  return waitForWiFi("OK", 200, 10);
}

int scanWiFi() {
    uBit.serial.send("AT+CWLAP\r\n", SYNC_SPINWAIT);
    return waitForWiFi("OK", 500, 50);
}

int modeWiFi(int mode) {
    ManagedString cmd="AT+CWMODE_CUR="+ManagedString(mode)+"\r\n";
    uBit.serial.send(cmd, SYNC_SPINWAIT);
    return waitForWiFi("OK", 200, 10);
}

int connectWiFi(ManagedString ssid, ManagedString pass) {
    ManagedString cmd = "AT+CWJAP_CUR=\""+ssid+"\",\""+pass+"\"\r\n";
    uBit.serial.send(cmd, SYNC_SPINWAIT);
    return waitForWiFi("OK", 200, 20);
}

int getIPWiFi() {
    uBit.serial.send("AT+CIFSR\r\n", SYNC_SPINWAIT);
    return waitForWiFi("OK", 200, 10);
}
```

```
int getWebPageWiFi(ManagedString URL, ManagedString page) {
  ManagedString cmd="AT+CIPSTART=\"TCP\",\""+URL+"\",80\r\n";
  uBit.serial.send(cmd, SYNC_SPINWAIT);
  if (waitForWiFi("OK", 100, 20) == 0) return 0;

  ManagedString http="GET "+page+"HTTP/1.0\r\nHost:"+URL+"\r\n\r\n";
  cmd = "AT+CIPSEND=" + ManagedString(http.length()) + "\r\n";
  uBit.serial.send(cmd, SYNC_SPINWAIT);
  int retry;
  ManagedString s;
  s = "";
  retry = 40;
  do {
      uBit.sleep(100);
      s = s + uBit.serial.read(500, ASYNC);
      retry--;
      } while (find(">", s) == 0 && retry != 0);

  uBit.serial.send(http, SYNC_SPINWAIT);
  retry = 100;
  do {
      uBit.sleep(100);
      s = s + uBit.serial.read(500, ASYNC);
      retry--;
    } while (s.length() < 500 && retry != 0);

  if (DEBUG)debug("\n\rPage\n\r" + s + "\n\r");
  return 1;
}

int startServerWiFi() {
    uBit.serial.send("AT+CIPMUX=1\r\n", SYNC_SPINWAIT);
    if (waitForWiFi("OK", 100, 20) == 0) return 0;

    uBit.serial.send("AT+CIPSERVER=1,80\r\n", SYNC_SPINWAIT);
    if (waitForWiFi("OK", 100, 20) == 0) return 0;

    ManagedString s;

    for (;;) {
        s="";
        do {
            uBit.sleep(100);
            if(s>500)s="";
            s = uBit.serial.read(500, ASYNC);
        } while (find("+IPD", s) == 0);
        if (DEBUG)debug("\n\rClient Connected\n\r" + s + "\n\r");
```

```
int b = find("+IPD", s);
        s = s.substring(b + 1, s.length());
        b = find(",", s);
        s = s.substring(b + 1, s.length());
        b = find(",", s);
        ManagedString id = s.substring(0, b);
        if (DEBUG)debug("\n\rTCP id:" + id + "\n\r");

        ManagedString headers = "HTTP/1.0 200 OK\r\n";
        headers = headers + "Server: micro:bit\r\n";
        headers = headers + "Content-type: text/html\r\n\r\n";

        ManagedString html ="<html><head><title>Temperature</title>
                             </head><body>{\"humidity\":81%,
                                \"airtemperature\":23.5C}</p>
                                        </body></html>\r\n";
        ManagedString data = headers + html;

        ManagedString cmd = "AT+CIPSEND=" + id + "," +
                             ManagedString(data.length()) + "\r\n";
        uBit.serial.send(cmd, SYNC_SPINWAIT);
        s = "";
        int retry = 40;
        do {
            uBit.sleep(100);
            s = s + uBit.serial.read(500, ASYNC);
            retry--;
        } while (find(">", s) == 0 && retry != 0);

        uBit.serial.send(data, SYNC_SPINWAIT);

        if (waitForWiFi("OK", 100, 100) == 0) return 0;
        if (DEBUG)debug("\n\rData Sent\n\r");

        cmd = "AT+CIPCLOSE=" + id + "\r\n";
        uBit.serial.send(cmd, SYNC_SPINWAIT);
        if (waitForWiFi("OK", 100, 100) == 0) return 0;
    }

}

void debug(ManagedString s) {
    uBit.serial.redirect(USBTX, USBRX);
    uBit.serial.send(s, SYNC_SPINWAIT);
    uBit.serial.redirect(Tx, Rx);
}
```

```
int find(ManagedString c, ManagedString s) {
    int i;

    for (i = 0; i < (s.length() - c.length()); i++) {
        if (c == s.substring(i, c.length())) break;
    }

    if (i == (s.length() - c.length())) return 0;
    return i;
}

int waitForWiFi(ManagedString target, int retry, int pause) {
    ManagedString s;
    do {
        uBit.sleep(pause);
        if(s.length()>500)s="";
        s = s + uBit.serial.read(500, ASYNC);
        retry--;
    } while (find(target, s) == 0 && retry != 0);
    if (DEBUG)debug("\n\r" + s + "\n\r");
    return retry;
}
```

# Chapter 14

# The LED Display

The micro:bit's LED display may only be 5x5 but it is very versatile. If you want to make use of it directly then you are going to have to master some lower level functions.

Mostly the functions provided by the framework are all you need to work with the LED display. They are also fairly self explanatory and easy to use so there is no point in going over them. You can look them up in the documentation and use them in programs without too much trouble. In this chapter we cover the structure of the LED display and some interesting ways of using it in the hope that you might find creative ways to use the display.

## Driving The LEDs

The basic structure of the LED array is fairly simple and obvious if you have ever done anything similar. The LEDs are arranged in a grid of three rows and five columns. Each row has a GPIO line to drive it and each row has a GPIO line that acts as ground or not depending on whether the LED should be on or off.

The arrangement of LEDs and GPIO lines is:

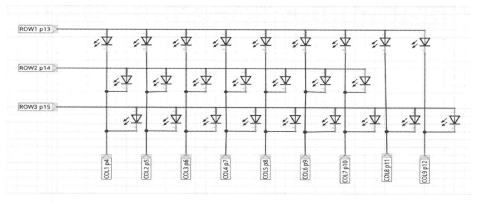

As you can see, there are two LEDs missing from the grid. If we had the full set of 3x9 LEDs we would have 27 while a 5x5 array only needs 25.

The GPIO assignments are:

```
LED MATRIX COLS
COL1 = p4
COL2 = p5
COL3 = p6
COL4 = p7
COL5 = p8
COL6 = p9
COL7 = p10
COL8 = p11
COL9 = p12
LED MATRIX ROWS
ROW1 = p13
ROW2 = p14
ROW3 = p15
```

The LEDs are also not arranged in a neat row/column numbering. Instead they are arranged in an order that makes the PCB layout easier:

| 1.1 | 2.4 | 1.2 | 2.5 | 1.3 |
|-----|-----|-----|-----|-----|
| 3.4 | 3.5 | 3.6 | 3.7 | 3.8 |
| 2.2 | 1.9 | 2.3 | 3.9 | 2.1 |
| 1.8 | 1.7 | 1.6 | 1.5 | 1.4 |
| 3.3 | 2.7 | 3.1 | 2.6 | 3.2 |

So to illuminate a given LED, i.e. one at position row.column, all we have to do is set the row GPIO high and the column GPIO low - this picks out just one LED to be on.

For example, to select the center LED 2,3 you would need to set GPIO line p14 high and line p6 low. The problem is that the framework only provides objects for GPIO lines that are brought out to the the edge connector and none of the row lines are and only some of the column lines are.

The solution is to make use of the mbed functions with which the framework is built. The disadvantage of this is that you don't get any of the event handling facilities. There are mbed functions for most of the hardware facilities that we have encountered and you can use them if you want to. They are slightly faster than the framework functions because in general the framework functions call the mbed functions to get the work done.

For example, to flash the middle LED we need a DigitalOut object from the mbed library.

| Function | Description |
| --- | --- |
| DigitalOut (PinName pin) | Create a DigitalOut connected to the specified pin |
| DigitalOut (PinName pin, int value) | Create a DigitalOut connected to the specified pin with given initial value |
| void write (int value) | Set the output, specified as 0 or 1 (int) |
| int read () | Return the output setting, represented as 0 or 1 (int) |
| int is_connected () | Return the output setting, represented as 0 or 1 (int) |
| DigitalOut & operator= (int value) | A shorthand for write() |
| operator int () | A shorthand for read() |

All you need to know to make use of this is that there is also a complete set of pin names like P0_n for GPIO Pin n. Using this you can access any GPIO line. In addition there are also predefined pin names for COL1 through COL9 and for ROW1, ROW2 and ROW3.

So to flash the center LED you would use:

```
#include "MicroBit.h"
MicroBit uBit;
int main() {
    uBit.init();
    uBit.display.disable();

    DigitalOut col3(P0_6,0);
    DigitalOut row2(P0_14);
    while(1) {
        row2 = 1;
        wait(0.2);
        row2 = 0;
        wait(0.2);
    }

    release_fiber();
    return 0;
}
```

Notice that to take control of the GPIO lines that work with the display you either have to not create the uBit object or you have to call the disable method of the display. After this the program simply sets col3 to zero and toggles row2 to flash the LED.

We could equally well have used:

```
    DigitalOut col3(COL3,0);
    DigitalOut row2(ROW2);
```

If you think about the hardware for a moment it should be obvious that we can turn on any LED in a single row by setting its row to on and multiple columns to off.

How then can we create a display where LEDs in different rows are on at the same time? The answer is that we turn then on an off so fast that the human eye can't see the flashing. For example to turn the LEDs on in column 3 and rows 1, 2 and 3 you could use:

```
DigitalOut col3(COL3,0);
DigitalOut row1(ROW1);
DigitalOut row2(ROW2);
DigitalOut row3(ROW3);
while(1) {
    row1 = 1;
    wait(0.2);
    row1 = 0;
    row2 = 1;
    wait(0.2);
    row2=0;
    row3 = 1;
    wait(0.2);
    row3=0;
}
```

If you run this program you will see the LEDs on the diagonal flash one after another. Now take out the wait function calls - you will see the three LEDs on the diagonal all apparently on at the same time.

This is what the framework display object does for you automatically. It scans the three rows turning on and off LEDs in that row to create a complete display. It is another job performed by the framework's event handling system.

If you want to do this sort of job at a reasonable speed you need to set and unset all of the LEDs in a single row in one operation as explained in the chapter on fast memory mapped GPIO. The mbed library has functions that you can use to do this or you can write your own.

## Greyscale

One of the features of the framework's support for the LED display that isn't so obvious is that you can use it as a greyscale display. The reason it isn't so obvious is that there isn't a setValue type function for a single LED. It doesn't have any functions that let you work with a single LED at all. However the display object uses a buffer which is a MicroBitImage object. The basic idea is that the render function displays what ever is in the buffer. You can create MicroBitImage objects and print them to the display or you can work directly with the buffer MicroBitImage object to display "live" graphics.

The key method is:

```
int setPixelValue( int16_t  x,int16_t  y,uint8_t value)
```

and the value can be anything from 0 to 255.

The brightness is created by simply turning the LED on and off in the correct ratio as in PWM, although PWM isn't used in the display. It is a simple consequence of the repeated rendering of the display and the percentage of time a pixel is set to on. For example you can slowly increase the brightness of the center LED:

```
uBit.init();
uBit.display.setDisplayMode(DISPLAY_MODE_GREYSCALE);
int i;
for(;;){
 for(i=0;i<256;i++){
    uBit.display.image.setPixelValue(2,2,i);
    uBit.sleep(50);
 }
}
```

Notice that you have to set the greyscale mode because this is more complex and hence not the default. You can explore the possibilities of using MicroBitImage object to perform animation and other graphical techniques. However the real problem is that no matter how clever your software you only have a 5x5 display.

## Using Aliasing to Increase Resolution

As an example of how you can use the grey level resolution of the display to increase its effective spatial resolution let's implement a traditional BBC Micro game - Commando Jump. This is a very simple game where a figure's height above the baseline is controlled by how fast the user clicks a button. Only showing the commando in five positions makes it a little crude.

As an alternative to simply moving the commando by one LED for every 10 button clicks, we can move the brightness from one to another gradually. You can think of this as locating the commando in the gaps between the LED, but it is also the standard anti-aliasing technique from higher resolution graphics.

A function to move the commando by fractional amounts is:

```
void flashMan(int x, int y, int p, int vx, int vy) {
    uBit.display.image.setPixelValue(x, y, 0);
    uBit.display.image.setPixelValue(x + vx, y + vy, 0);
    uBit.sleep(100);
    uBit.display.image.setPixelValue(x, y, 25 * (10 - p));
    uBit.display.image.setPixelValue(x + vx, y + vy, 25 * p);
    uBit.sleep(100);
}
```

The commando is at x,y and p is used to indicate how close it is to being at x+vx and y+vy. For example, suppose p is 0 then the first LED is set to 10*25, i.e. 250, and the second to 0. If p is 3 then the first is set to 7*25 and the second to 3*25. Finally is p is 10 the first is set to 0 and the second to 10*25. As p varies from 0 to 10 the position of the brightness moves from the first to the second LED.

We also need something to record how many times the button has been clicked. This can be done using an event handler that counts clicks using a global variable. There is no doubt that this would be better implemented as an object using C++ with methods such as getValue and reset and so on, but in C we use:

```
void setUpButton() {
    uBit.buttonB.setEventConfiguration(MICROBIT_BUTTON_ALL_EVENTS);
    uBit.messageBus.listen(MICROBIT_ID_BUTTON_B,
                    MICROBIT_BUTTON_EVT_CLICK,
                    buttonClickCount);
}
```

Now buttonClickCount is called each time the user clicks buttonB:

```
void buttonClickCount(MicroBitEvent e) {
    clickCount++;
}
```

Now we have all of the elements needed to implement the game.

# Commando Jump Program

```
#include "MicroBit.h"

MicroBit uBit;
int clickCount = 0;

void startGame();
int playGame();
void endGame(int position);void countDown();
void drawPlayArea();
void flashMan(int x, int y, int p, int vx, int vy);
void setUpButton();
void moveHorizontal();
void moveVertical(int x, int h);
void buttonClickCount(MicroBitEvent e);

int main() {
 uBit.init();
 startGame();
 int position = playGame();
 endGame(position);
 release_fiber();
 return 0;
}

void startGame() {
 countDown();
 uBit.display.setDisplayMode(DISPLAY_MODE_GREYSCALE);
 drawPlayArea();
 setUpButton();
}

void countDown() {int t;
 for (t = 5; t >= 0; t--) {
  uBit.display.scroll(t);
 }
 uBit.display.scroll("!");
}

void drawPlayArea() {
 uBit.display.clear();
 int y;
 for (y = 1; y <= 5; y++) {
  uBit.display.image.setPixelValue(2, y, 255);
 }
}
```

```
int playGame() {
 int position = 4;
 clickCount = 0;
 int t1 = uBit.systemTime();

 while (uBit.systemTime() - t1 < 20000) {
   flashMan(4,  position, clickCount, 0, -1);
   if (clickCount > 10) {
     position = position - 1;
     clickCount = 0;
     if (position == 0)break;
   }
 }
 return position;
}

void endGame(int position) {
 if (position == 0) {
  moveHorizontal();
  moveVertical(0, 0);
 } else {
  moveVertical(4, position);
 }
}

void setUpButton() {
 uBit.buttonB.setEventConfiguration(MICROBIT_BUTTON_ALL_EVENTS);
 uBit.messageBus.listen(MICROBIT_ID_BUTTON_B,
                    MICROBIT_BUTTON_EVT_CLICK,
                    buttonClickCount);
}

void buttonClickCount(MicroBitEvent e) {
 clickCount++;
}

void flashMan(int x, int y, int p, int vx, int vy) {
 uBit.display.image.setPixelValue(x, y, 0);
 uBit.display.image.setPixelValue(x + vx, y + vy, 0);
 uBit.sleep(100);
 uBit.display.image.setPixelValue(x, y, 25 * (10 - p));
 uBit.display.image.setPixelValue(x+vx, y+vy, 25*p);
 uBit.sleep(100);
}

void moveHorizontal() {
 int x, fraction;
 for (x = 4; x >= 0; x--) {
  for (fraction = 0; fraction <= 10; fraction++) {
   flashMan(x, 0, fraction, -1, 0);
  }
```

```
    }
}

void moveVertical(int x, int h) {
  int y, fraction;
  if (h != 0)
    uBit.display.image.setPixelValue(x, h - 1, 0);
    for (y = h; y <= 4; y++) {
      for (fraction = 0;
        fraction <= 10; fraction++) {
        flashMan(x, y, fraction, 0, 1);
      }
    }
}
```

If you try it out you will discover that the use of greyscale to increase the resolution works well, but it works even better if you scale the LED brightness using a power law as given in Chapter 5 with reference to pulse width modulation

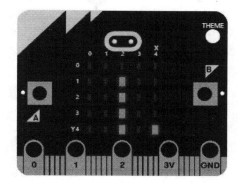

I don't think that the 5x5 display is going to be hosting an implementation of Doom any time soon, but who knows!

# Index

Made in the USA
Lexington, KY
06 February 2018